Eleven Jour

Megalith:

Eleven Journeys
in Search of Stones

Edited by
Damian Walford Davies

Gomer

Published in 2006 by
Gomer Press, Llandysul, Ceredigion SA44 4JL
www.gomer.co.uk

ISBN 1 84323 665 6
ISBN-13 9781843236658
A CIP record for this title is available from the British Library

This book is published with the financial support of the
Welsh Books Council.

Printed and bound in Wales at
Gomer Press, Llandysul, Ceredigion

CONTENTS

PREFACE

To my mind the splendour of megaliths lies in their infinite variety – not physical variety, because visually they tend towards sameness, most of them being vaguely rectangular of component, and all being made of stone – but inner variety, as it were.

In this they have the advantage that nobody knows what they are, or what they were for. We can rely upon no archaeologists' expertise or scholars' exegesis, because they are really no better informed than we are ourselves. This means that we can read the old stones as we will, finding our own meanings in them, and interpreting their presences, as our forefathers did down the ages, in all manner of fable, symbolism or mumbo-jumbo.

For myself I sometimes find them rather entertaining – like the prehistoric stone maze at Visby, on the Baltic island of Gotland, which provides fun for one and all to this very day, or the cromlech that crouches near the stables of Plas Newydd in Wales, the ancestral mansion of the Marquesses of Anglesey, perpetually cocking a snook at circumstance. Sometimes I am comforted by them. There is a standing stone near my house in Gwynedd, almost unnoticed in a field, which has been my good friend for many years, if only because its mottled boulder secretes for me a sweet and unmistakable smell of donkey. This is impossible – no donkey has ever been near the place – but in the misty world of the megaliths, anything can be true.

Of course, enigma is part of the charm. What a joy to know that there are still matters beyond the ken of science or religion! It is this that gives the megaliths, all around the world, their sense of immemorial power. They are like faceless visitors from another universe, more potent by far than any sphinx or slave-built pyramid. Did anybody really make these things? We cannot know, but they frequently seem to me, if not actually animate, then certainly formidably sensate – incalculably older than we are, and probably much wiser, too.

On the other hand there is something baleful to them. On gloomy days they can be disquieting. The fairies who used to frequent them were not always sprites of sweet nature, but often malevolent sorcerers, kidnappers or revengers. So I have often felt the stones themselves to be – always there, always seeing us, waiting, judging, keeping an Orwellian watch upon us all. There is an eerie inscription on a stone near my home which gives me a shudder: *Y Garreg a Lefa o'r Mur*, it simply says, The Stone Cries from the Wall . . .

In other moods, at other times, I am depressed by megaliths. They can look cheerful enough in the sunshine, amiable in bright morning light, but when they stand silent in the rain they sometimes seem to me utterly numb. Then they suggest to me images of death, and not death of the body either, but death of the soul – absolute death, all life forgotten, warmth or cold, sun or drizzle all unfelt.

And now and then I feel sorry for the megaliths. Haunting, comic, scary, consoling, they can also be pitiable. The saddest stones I know are the wizened menhir-statues called the Paladins, in a muddy field near the sea in Corsica, thought by some to be portraits of prehistoric heroes. They may have been commanding once, high above the brambles there, but millennia of sea-winds have given them an arthritic, complaining look, tempering not only their authority but also their arcanum.

I sympathise with them – they seem to me like hypochondriac senior citizens, whimpering to us across the ages – but the Paladins probably don't feel like that at all. They probably feel on top of the world. Their pathos is only in my mind, for by the nature of things the megalithic stones are above all allegories of the imagination; and the imagination being an instrument of infinite variety, it seems to me that the essays in this book, written out of such varied resources of learning, observation, fantasy and not least poetical instinct, possess in themselves a grandly megalithic quality.

JAN MORRIS

Writing Stones

Damian Walford Davies

Megaliths: big stones, especially (the dictionary tells us) those forming part of a prehistoric monument. Call them dolmens, cromlechs, barrows, quoits, menhirs, standing stones, monoliths; think of them as the unsung masterpieces of Neolithic and Bronze-Age construction – communal buildings, architecture for the dead, calendars, solstice-trackers, maps, stages, performance spaces, works of art. See how they are rooted in a landscape, growths of a particular ground. Consider them as paradoxes – stonily alive, their delicate tonnage dynamically stationary. Notice how each has an identity, a bearing, peculiar to itself.

Centuries after their construction, their original purpose lost, they became baffling presences. But people always sought some imaginative purchase on their barefaced stoniness. Myth claimed them. They were exoticised, made forbiddingly other, given names such as The Ship of Death, The Devil's Quoit, The Water Monster's Grave. They were also naturalised: 'Long Meg, Five Kings, Nine Maidens,/ Twelve Apostles: with such familiar names/ We make them part of ordinary lives', as John Ormond put it in 'Ancient Monuments'. The antiquarians delivered them from fables of giants, saints, devils and monstrous prodigies, only to embalm them anew in the cooked mysteries of druidic lore. The archaeologists dug deep, sometimes obliterating, always excavating as many questions as answers. And then, suddenly, the megaliths became our monumental 'heritage' – railed off, signposted, policed on midsummer morning, mute witnesses to the fraught politics of conservation.

Let us explode another myth: it is not just the neo-pagans, New Agers and modern mystics who now incline towards the megaliths. These deadpan deadweights have always commanded a varied demographic. For modern megalithomaniacs, the resonance of the stones transcends the dryly antiquarian and the shamanistically *outré*. Megaliths are not 'monuments', open-air museum pieces, but living topographical features exerting an irresistible pull. Far from being the atavistic obsession of the odd and dysfunctional, the five-and-a-half-thousand-year-old cromlech tombs and the younger, three-and-a-half-thousand-year-old menhirs, stone circles and alignments have proved utterly relevant and contemporary. Not anachronistic but cutting-edge. These sites offer a salutary lengthening of historical perspective in an age obsessed with the quick fix. They remain the locus of spiritual access and ecological insight; they are whetstones that sharpen social and political vision. Megaliths may stand in stark contrast to our technological, speeding selves and to our increasingly megalopolitan existence, but for those who seek them out, they rarely offer an escape into a pastoral otherworld. Rather, they've proved adept at focusing the complexities and tensions of modern life. They are mirrors, reflecting us back in various forms. In their lichened, faceted faces we see our lineaments; in their solitariness, our loneliness, or our need to be alone; in their gregariousness, our congregational temper; in their alignment, our deviousness; in their poised mass, our fragility; in their rootedness, our deracination; in their age, our ephemerality; and in their naked outfacing of time and the elements, a valuable lesson in patient dissent. And yet most of us speed past them, or are unaware of their existence.

And what was once stone is now plastic. The peripatetic *eisteddfod* festival used to leave its nouveau-megalithic signature annually on its host town in the form of a folly: a stone circle in which the mummeries of the *gorsedd* – the *eisteddfod*'s ritual heart – are solemnly performed. New megaliths are no longer an option; since 2005, the cash-strapped neo-Neolithic builders of Wales have opted for plastic, portable stones – the products of Vinamold® hot melt moulding compound and Jesmonite acrylic. When John Ormond declared 'Some monuments move', he didn't mean this. (Jesmonite, according to one website, 'is free of toxic fumes. It is acoustically dead. It is therefore eminently suitable for shopping malls, airports and other public spaces'.) The artists who made the plastic megaliths also specialise in garden sculpture and film props. There's a certain rightness, as well as absurdity, to this: the original megalith-builders also possessed a keen sense of drama, an alertness to the effect of place and light and form on an audience – dead, as well as living. From stone to synthetic material, megaliths move with the times.

'Yesterday', said Auden, 'the diffusion/ Of the counting-frame and the cromlech.' Today, that diffusion proceeds in virtual space with the proliferation of websites gazetteering the megaliths, from *The Stone Circle Webring* and *Megalithic Walks* to *Stone Pages* and *The Megalithic Portal*. But the language of the web is that of the ancient stones: site, ring, portal. The new technologies are aligned with the old.

Despite the best efforts of the archaeologists, anthropologists and scientists, so much about the megaliths remains a puzzle. Their mass thwarts the conviction that we know, and can explain, everything. A cromlech's frame, denuded of its covering mound or cairn, ultimately resists interpretation. Despite its unequivocal thisness, a standing stone stolidly defies domestication. We can get to them, but cannot get at them. This resistance is their great glory and attraction. Witness Louis MacNeice's linking of lovers and cromlechs in a poem warning against 'Extracters and abstracters' who murder to dissect:

> Tom is here, Tessy is here
> At this point in a given year
> With all this hour's accessories,
> A given glory – and to look
> That gift-horse in the mouth will prove

Or disprove nothing of their love,
Which is as sure intact a fact,
Though young and supple, as what stands
Obtuse and old, in time congealed,
Behind them as they mingle hands –
Self-contained, unexplained,
The cromlech in the clover field.

The young lovers' love is as incontrovertibly itself – as powerfully, mysteriously there – as the dolmen behind them, which in turn, though 'obtuse and old', partakes of a measure of their youth, suppleness and mingling. The stone grave is a site for the contemporary imagination to dig in.

*   *   *

In this book, eleven writers offer compelling engagements with eleven megalithic sites. From Dumfries and Galloway to the Isles of Scilly, these essays remap Scottish, Irish, Welsh and English ground. The result of some fascinating fieldwork, these creative non-fiction travelogues pitched towards stone conflate the ancient and urgent, drawing nature-writing, life-writing, history and (psycho)geography into illuminating alignment. Gesturing at ways in which we might orientate and orienteer ourselves anew, the journeys profiled here are contemporary pilgrimages of a radical kind – travel-writing with a difference. Charting emotional, spiritual and historical odysseys into the past, present and future, into landscapes both external and internal, public and private, these narratives offer memorable portraits of both ancient stones and modern stone haunters, who take their place in a venerable tradition of stone-writing. I invited each writer to choose a site that resonated in some personal way. The result is a book in which cold stone and emotional experience are dramatically linked.

How does one write stones? That depends, of course, on the stone in question. Each essay in this collection is differently attuned to its stony subject, as the authors excavate a range of styles and voices to gain access to a particular megalithic site. The link between stones and words, between the texture of megaliths and the contours of language, is a recurrent concern. To write about megaliths is to write around them, and the stones act as gravitational centres or points of departure for wider meditations; associative ley-lines radiate out from the megaliths in all directions. The essays communicate with one another in suggestive ways, each a component stone in the volume's alignment (or circle, or dolmen). In addition, it is impossible to consider megaliths without contemplating the landscape they inhabit – and our responsibility towards it. In this sense, an ecological stratum runs through the volume. There is playfulness in these fieldnotes, too; after all, a 'quoit' is something thrown in a game, and so many of these stones are said to have been hurled into place by ancient strongmen, as in some petrific olympics.

Six of the sites are Neolithic; five are Bronze-Age. For the authors of *Megalith*, they are far more than mere conglomerations of stone. Jim Perrin's essay is both a powerful statement about rites and rights and a moving personal document. Celebrated here is the 'essential littleness of our knowledge' about his Scottish stones; this is a writer thrilled by the absence of information, who sets a sort of wise passiveness against what he sees as the damage wrought by dogma and by aggressive appropriation (of individuals, as of stones). Associated with the various Irish stones in Bernard O'Donoghue's essay are accident and violence (suffered by both megaliths and men), potent absent presences, and those disturbing slippages between 'irrational belief' and 'rational history' that continue to haunt our encounters with these objects, inflecting our notions of time. Tristan Hughes's vistas across his chosen burial chamber on Anglesey take in stoniness and fecundity, movement and stillness, past, present and future tourists, and notions of continued habitation. At the heart of the piece is an act of sympathetic imagining – a sketch of a disaffected man who came to sketch the stones and who may, or may not, have found solace there.

A layered landscape is explored through the layered language of allusion in Andrew McNeillie's essay. Like the stones of his platform cairn, those allusions (to Vaughan, Wordsworth, Hopkins, Yeats, Gurney, Dylan Thomas, MacDiarmid, Ted Hughes, Geoffrey Hill, and McNeillie's own poetry) are variously located for the reader to excavate: some on the surface, some embedded, some compacted. The voice avoids the lapidary, ranging from the lyrical to the ludic as the stones are approached from different angles. Seasonal variations on stone: this is how Niall Griffiths approaches two Welsh monoliths, drawing into their odd orbit small and large 'carnage', physical and psychological trauma, hearsay and spun stories, and, finally, survival. The accretions and compressions of memory occupy Gillian Clarke as she considers essential stoniness and the intersection of private and public myths and histories. Clarke constructs the great cromlech at Pentre Ifan anew through the layering of prose and poetry.

My own encounter with a Welsh stone row in The Field of the Dead is an exercise in transhistorical imagination that seeks to bring the field's traumatic strata alive. Orbiting the megaliths, I tune into various transmissions, ancient and modern, in order to align the stones with contemporary technology. In play here are digressions, repetitions, misdirections, views and rearviews, inclines and descents, conjunctions, patinas – computed in twos, threes and quads, and always disturbed by traces of violence. Menna Elfyn captures her megalith in seventeen pared-down vignettes – lyrical snapshots that play with the 'touristic'. Maen Ceti becomes a focus in 'restless' technological times for a consideration of inter-generational relations, language and cultural identity, burial, and acts of literal and imaginative lifting. For Elin ap Hywel, the massive stones of Tinkinswood are part of a delicate effort to imagine an uncle known only through photographs. Again, we are confronted with a world of accident and violence; a cromlech serves once more as the juncture of prehistory and family history, of ancient inhumation and twentieth-century bereavement. Pondered here is the weight of our own buried lives.

A Gloucestershire long barrow gives former archaeologist Jem Poster the opportunity to unearth a past self. Sensitively negotiating conservation and intrusion, the claims of archaeology and the imagination, Poster asks us to consider the problems of interpreting these sites. He is interested in the ways in which megaliths are recorded, drawn, written up, dressed down, recovered and re-covered. Disturbance and salutary 'terror' are at the heart of his return journey. The final piece by David Constantine takes an island tomb as a platform for a meditation on the coexistence and codependence of the living and the dead. A hill on the Isles of Scilly becomes shifting, paradoxical ground; the author is alive to the 'agitated quickness' of water and the static liveliness of stone, knowing the place to be a locus of creative 'florescence' where time is fundamentally collapsed and all things are 'coeval'.

Megalith: Eleven Journeys in Search of Stones is an inspired ordnance survey. The collection offers a new kind of cartography, one that maps not only stony structures and the contours of precious landscapes, but dramatic emotional and psychological terrain. The (pre)historical vistas opened up in these essays illuminate contemporary predicaments. For those who frequent stones and navigate by them, the megaliths are potent receivers through which one tunes into pressing modern frequencies.

APPROPRIATIONS

The Drumtroddan Stones, Dumfries and Galloway, Scotland

Jim Perrin

Between events at a literary festival, not wanting the chatter, resisting the attempts to own, I sneak away in search of some more substantial and silent thing, and drive mapless along twisting roads until a sign for the stones points me down a muddy avenue, its one margin impenetrable thicket, its other a row of beech trees maybe two centuries old, stately in their decay. Autumn has tinted but not yet stripped the leaves and mast crisps the ground. An even wash of light across the sky is that reflected one of proximity to water. The lane debouches into a wide, sloping field irregularly sectioned with electrified cord. Friesian heifers with tagged ears chase up to me to gaze and huff. A high mortarless wall marks the boundary between pasture and woodland. Not so much as a scratching post for kine stands proud of the soft brae. Suspicious of absence, I search the wall itself for clues – the long slabs rooting against land's inclination, the slivers knapped to inclusion, even the suggestion of a face in bas-relief on a flat plane. As geology, geomorphology, history dispose, so does man – attentive to immediate need alone – re-use. Marks and motifs have been re-incorporated down the centuries, a recycled jumble of stone. A long circuit in bovine company and I conclude that what I'm looking for is at best only hinted at here, turn on my heel, and there, half-a-mile away across the road, a monument, prominent on the farther hill-crest. The sign had been turned mischievously away.

Grass of the field I now cross has smoothed the turned clod only to a casual eye. The plough has thrown its share of hidden stumbles before the stones of Drumtroddan. There are three of them along a low ridge, two uprights in approximate south-west to north-east alignment and another that lies prone close to the southerly standing stone. The rock is greywacke – resistant, sound, thinly-bedded, crystalline-pebbled, silvery-pink and covered with sage-green and lemony lichen. This landscape of the Isle of Whithorn in Galloway where the stones are to be found is rolling and copsed – good, rich acres, a teardrop of fertility weeping out of the barren highlands to the north into the Solway Firth, its land-encircled sea invisible from here.

I contemplate the shape of the stones. The uprights are, I would guess, forty feet apart and about ten feet in height. The northern one is hairier – more lichenous and more slender, like a shaped and hooked blade. The southern one tilts, is top-heavy, less elegant, and has been drilled at some time in the last century or two, perhaps for use as a gatepost. A stump close to it is clearly that on which the third megalith stood, weathered fracture-lines consonant on rooted fragment and prone stone. Barbed wire surrounds the monument; a wicket gate of metal gives access to the enclosure. The minimal sign placed here by Historic Scotland conjectures its age as three or four millennia, which locates it in the early to middle Bronze Age. Beyond that, the text on the board admits mystery, and ignorance of any further knowledge as to date, purpose, fact. As I walk away, I glance back to see the stones set and enduring against a slate-grey sky. A drift of fine rain darkens the corbelled field-walls.

Beyond Drumtroddan Farm are the cup-and-ring marks. They're clustered, dozens in sum, on two *roches moutonnées* in a field, and on a third in a copse of ash and willow beyond. For the most part they're a small hand's-breadth across, though some are two or three times this size, and comprise two concentric incised circles around a shallow round dish in the rock. A few, in promiscuous alignments, have a line incised through rings to bowl, rough-textured as images from microscopy of sperm fertilizing ova. Another Historic Scotland sign again gives their purpose as unknown. A spotted calf grazes calmly nearby. I leave to drive south with a sense of quiet delight at the lack of information recorded here.

And then begin to ruminate, and to talk with people about them, and by way of information am given not much, and that little spiralling back to certain salient, minimal facts. Relating to the carvings first. No-one knows what the cup-and-ring marks signify. The believers in earth magic fixate on an undoubted similarity to the Cretan Maze – a design repeatedly curling back on itself so that solving the riddle of core-access involves a sequence of rings, each directing you back around the next ring in decreasing circles towards – it's hoped – a Minotaur-free centre. New-Age belief holds just such a maze to be laid out around Glastonbury Tor, circling and recircling as you climb gradually upwards to reach the ruined chapel at the top. To follow it exactly at midnight under the full moon would bring you to a door into the Underworld – a tenet perhaps not vastly more far-fetched than some of the central ones of Christianity, and in the event much more likely to lead to an encounter with a gang of amiable hippies contentedly sucking on their spliffs than to the descent into Hell. The most common assumption about the cup-and-ring marks – one that runs the gamut from serious academic archaeologists to New-Age pundits – is that the cup represents the sun, the concentric circles the cycles of the seasons, the act of carving itself being supplicatory or propitiatory to the gods in whatever guise they were then deemed to exist. At the extreme end of the interpretative spectrum come comments like this:

> There is an affinity between these cups and the nature of the stars. A star is a generator and transmitter of Cosmic Energy in spiral form. These cups could be used as microcosmic examples of spiral-staral energies.

So, we are stardust, and who am I to gainsay the notion that prehistoric man lived with and celebrated an awareness of the fractal nature of the universe, its patterns imprinting ever more grandly, ever more minutely on human consciousness? What I am aware of, from my own travels and reading, is that the symbols occur across Europe. They are on tombs – on a much-photographed kerbstone at Newgrange in Ireland in association with other diamond, lozenge and spiral patterns; or better still at Locmariquer near the great stone rows of Carnac in Brittany. On other rocks unhidden from the sky you come upon them, even in the Scandinavian fringe of the Arctic. There is a fine cup-marking on a boulder in Malmo which must have originated well to the north of where it now rests. A rare one was incised into a stone at Avebury – rare because they are not often to be found on the great henge monuments and megalithic alignments of Europe's seaboard. I like the essential littleness of our knowledge about things important to a time preceding ours: megaliths as teeth set in the earth's skull, snapping at a net of stars; complex, carved designs that may map the journey to a place of which we can no longer conceive.

Of Drumtroddan, the received wisdom is that the middle stone was pushed down during the Early Christian era by colonising monks who were followers of Saint Ninian, the latter having built a stone church, *Candida Casa* – The White House – hereabouts, late in the fourth century according to Bede of Jarrow. This casual underpinning of the conjectural with the historically factual causes me to shake my head benignly at the ways of humankind. The assertions are blandly and unexaminedly based on much later historical examples – the destruction by a zealous eighteenth-century clergyman of stones at Avebury, for example; or even the attempt within very recent decades of a Church in Wales clergyman to have cut down an avenue of ancient yew trees in the circular *temenos* at Llangadwaladr – an avenue the first origins of which perhaps owe more to the nearby Bronze-Age tumulus than to the Christian era. As to Drumtroddan, there is no scrap of specific and local historical evidence to suggest that the central stone was deliberately toppled, and the flaws of geology itself point to that far more common vandal, time. But the notion does set my mind oscillating between the twin poles of appropriation and destruction. We know for certain that acts of religiously motivated historical vandalism took place at Avebury, and that they were as extreme and dire in their effect as much that happened during the Dissolution of the Monasteries. We might wander down the stately, columnar grove which is Tewkesbury Abbey's nave and look at relict tracery beyond the altar, the delicate, intricate beauty of which was smashed by Roundhead zealots. We might make common cause between these and the fallen stone of Drumtroddan. Or we might assume instead that the *peregrini*, steeped in triads, soaking up symbol as readily as the salt spray of their voyagings, would more likely have envisioned the Christian Trinity in these sun-aligned stones, would have appropriated rather than sought to destroy, and might even have thought to carve images on this granular, easy rock in their own faith's likenesses, as present-day monumental masons, unattuned to ancient resonance, offer quartz chips for scattering on graves of the computer age. Out on Caher Island off County Mayo, at the remote and utter abeyant end of the Croagh Patrick pilgrimage route, I have seen megaliths shaped roughly into the symbol of the cross, white boulders at their feet. Assimilated . . .

The mazeyness of human response is at issue here, when faced with mystery. Megaliths have some clearly observable characteristics in common, telling us a certain amount – and no more than that – about cultures that left no written records. As with Jung's mandalas, as with fractals, patterns recur. And careful archaeologists have unearthed yet more suggestive evidence for possible usages: the proliferation of post-holes along azimuths which would have aligned with stones and significant stars in Neolithic times is a feature common to many of the great monuments, so that *Regulus, Bella, Sirius, Capella* and *Vega* come into the megalithic orbit as clearly as Jesus, Mary and Joseph into the Christian, and their historicity and continuing existence is far more easily proven:

There have been many attempts to read astronomical significance into megalithic monuments and to endow them with remarkable mathematical sophistication. Some of what has been written is completely spurious and some is unproven. Yet there remains the unshakeable fact that a number of our most impressive megalithic tombs were designed with immense skill to relate precisely to significant solar or lunar events.

That's Professor Barry Cunliffe in *Facing the Ocean* (2001), and he goes on to cite the examples of Newgrange, Maes Howe and Gavr'inis, the midsummer or midwinter sun illuminating their recesses, so that light for once is shed on a mystery. But it is of the essence of organised religion that the mystery is retained: to recruit initiates; to exclude; to maintain power and control. How little the politico-religious storytellers have left in common between Yeshua of Nazareth, rabbi and homilist, and the theological Jesus Christ; and how insistent they are on mediated contact with a divinity rather than the mysticism and oneness of the Gnostics; and how viciously do our present-day Pharisees of Christian fundamentalism round on the latter, thus betraying their own distance from The Word.

Once, after the death of one I most dearly loved, I saw the little lilac helium balloon that had been tied to the steel frame of a hospital bed during her last days released into the still air of a calm spring evening. Courting redstarts were flitting among goat willow and the branches of a sycamore as the balloon rose straight up for fifty feet and then took off due west across the moors on an unwavering course at great speed. At the exact point and moment of its disappearance from sight, a star came out, blinked once, and was gone. There were other people present, but they were oblivious, regarding each other and themselves, and did not witness this happen, since for the most part we have lost the capacity to see. For me, it was an event of astonishment and magic and resonates still. Looking westwards across the moor in the void beyond my wife's death, what I experienced, momentarily, was innocent consciousness – balloon, trajectory, star, the notion and possibility of a soul journeying had become one.

Of course, there is a puzzle here, and it was brought home to me most starkly in succeeding days. Not only with this good woman's death, but with those of other persons whom I have loved. Repeatedly, I have noticed how death's horrors are inflicted posthumously. False certainty, assertion, ownership clamour at the heels of death: a doctor, maybe – some self-assured and authoritarian general practitioner, unused to having his word questioned, who will lecture dogmatically on consciousness, about which the best scientists know little; a western Buddhist, perhaps, who will yelp at, and place ritual objects around, a corpse in homage to an alien and unassimilated tradition which he alone, among those present, upholds; or adult children who seek to infantilise a departed parent in their memorialisings, in order to assert sole and exclusive claim. All these are more or less ignorant attempts to appropriate and control, all of them unworthy of their objects and unheeding of the enduring mystery. Yes, surely, as human beings we must *enquire*, as the raisers of megaliths observed and enquired of the rotation of the heavens, millennia ago; but also, and as surely, we must still ourselves into an acceptance of the unknowable (into which, always, further knowledge may yet enter).

It is in their mystery that the charge of the megaliths lies. They, too, are beyond death. All that we know of them is what remains of them – they are time's ruins, subject to a process of slow decay. Imagine them painted or bedecked. Imagine processions passing through, rich rituals, wooden structures around them. More happened here than we can now see; more happens here than we can see, as the ultrasonic scanning of the Dragon Project undertaken in the late 1970s revealed. The stones of Drumtroddan were not raised to be three lonely monoliths, arbitrary, the middle one collapsed. Clearly they were purposive, but we need to accept that our understanding is relict, in counterpoint to the surviving evidence of stone. What can help? Story? Is that not always dangerous in human terms, as exemplified in the case of

Christianity? Who have been the repositories, and what were their agendas? Even the oral tradition of the eternally watching peasant is subject to influence, and is seldom pure in transcription. Yet the distorting echoes possess their own power. Here's a good example, from one of the most resonant of English stone circles – Mitchell's Fold, right on the Shropshire–Powys border and in a landscape the mood of which Mary Webb (a storyteller whose manipulations are those perfectly straightforward ones necessary to fiction) evokes in her description of the adjacent Stiperstones:

> A mass of quartzite, blackened and hardened by unaccountable ages. The scattered rocks, the rugged holly-brakes on the lower slopes were like small carved lions beside the marble steps of a stupendous throne. Nothing ever altered its look. Dawn quickened over it in pearl and emerald; summer sent the armies of heather to its very foot; snow rested there as doves nest in cliffs. It remained inviolable, taciturn, evil. It glowered darkly on the dawn; it came through the snow like jagged bones through flesh; before its hardness even the venturesome cranberries were discouraged. For miles around in the plains, the valleys, the mountain dwellings it was feared. It drew the thunder, people said. Storms broke round it suddenly out of a clear sky; it seemed almost as if it created storm. No one cared to cross the range near it after dark – when the black grouse laughed sardonically and the cry of a passing curlew shivered like broken glass.

If that has not sufficiently unsettled you, the mood of the place finds further expression in Shropshire's own version of the European folktale motif of *The Wild Hunt* – led in its incarnation here by an eleventh-century Mercian thane who has transmuted into Wild Edric. With his scaly-tailed demon-band, to view which is to die, he shrieks, howls, swarms and swoops over the Stiperstones to signify impending war. I first came to Mitchell's Fold by way of the Stiperstones in just such a time – Bush and Blair in full cry against The Infidel – one snowy Epiphany, the sun westering and making all the miniature globes of ice embroidered into the heather glint like pearls. When I had gained the bridleway along Stapeley Hill, frost-diamonds feathered the quiffs of blond grass and caught at the afterlight, the day fading fast, the snowy track a glimmer. Corndon Hill's great bulk ahead, I raced along in gathering night, hill-shapes and the creak of my footsteps across the snow for company, skated across frozen flashes, and came to the dip in the hill which is Mitchell's Fold. The stone circle here once had perhaps as many as thirty uprights. Now there are fifteen, the largest of them the height of a tall man. The story told about these stones runs thus: in bad times long ago, people were hungry and all they had to depend on was a fairy cow who came here night and morning to be milked. There was always enough for all, so long as everyone took only one pail. Never more than one pail for each – on that the story is quite clear. But a witch came and milked the cow into a sieve until she ran dry, went away, and was never seen again. In the folktale, a giant owned the cow, and he was so angry at her loss he turned the witch into a stone, and all the other stones were put up round her to keep her in place.

You scarcely need a working knowledge of the role of the cow in Celtic mythology to deconstruct this story. Shadows of the old gods are here. As Alan Garner wrote of a similar Cheshire folktale in one of his essays, 'It is in its present manifestation a Celtic cosmos, not an English one. It is old, and it is alive'.

The story gives us a way to approach megaliths. Reverence – open-hearted and open-minded – is the key, is the opposite of appropriation and is an aspect of love, which is, in the essential Gnostic formulation, God. So our reverence is for the source, whether we view it as grey-bearded, crouched and wielding dividers, or simply as stardust and mystery. At Mitchell's Fold I stood in the night, leaning against a restraining upright, looking up at the stars. To the south, silvery, rose the thinnest sickle moon, and a phrase of Hölderlin's occurred to me as inscription –

immer
Ins Ungebundene gehet eine Sehnsucht.

– 'a longing always towards the Infinite'. Christianity, complicit down the ages and even in the present in the slaughter of millions, has lost all claim to purity in that. But perhaps, divorced from power, bereft of coercive ritual, what is left of the megaliths, like the 'bare, ruin'd choirs' of the great monasteries, can embody that yearning.

I remember sleeping on a stony riverbank in the rainforest of Sarawak, watching men in the dawn cast stone-weighted nets into the water to catch small, spiny fish which they cooked over an open fire, the bones numerous and pricking, the flesh meagre. Thus with dogma, faith, and belief. Why drag down the stars of wonder, attentiveness and love?

On the shortest day, a stillness in me at the prospect of light's return, I decided to seek out my favourite stone circle. In drenching weather and beneath dark clouds I made my way south of the Berwyn – the white barrier – to Pistyll Rhaeadr, highest of Welsh waterfalls and the most positively atmospheric. The little river, Afon Disgynfa, that plunges over the lip to become in that point of departure Afon Rhaeadr, was in spate, jets of water mingling to plunge directly on to the mysterious natural bridge below the main fall, through which a further torrent gouted forth, braiding into the cascade which was tinged with peat so that the whole fall became like heavy flaxen hair that was turning to white, like some emanation of the goddess. It made me think of standing on the footbridge at Beltane three years previously, the pistyll then in equal spate, and my wife's hand in mine, fingers as sweetly entwined.

Like sodden hanks of fleece the grasses on either side of the fall hung lankly down, their texture somehow predominating within the scene, as though all the flooding rush of time were somehow subsumed into the fixed and subdued. I turned from all that fall to the path through the wood. Chaffinches flitted around, and the leaves of beech and birch, still in December surprisingly thick on the boughs, were pale lemon, burnt orange, even a crinkled and glossy green. Wherever I looked, what my eye came to dwell upon was a rich, saturated, mature intensity of colour which owed nothing to spring's vivacity or summer's fullness. Over by Cerrig Poethion across Nant y Llyn the bracken was umber; on Braich y Gawres – the arm of the giantess – it was a dense maroon. And as I walked past the first of the ancient cairns in the long valley above the waterfall, I felt glad that it was winter, and therefore the time when the bracken has died back, revealing the features of the landscape; but at the same time I was fixing my attention in a kind of ecstasy on what it added to the scene. A north wind whipped the cutting, cold rain from the high Berwyn into my face, and allowed no comfort here. I slipped down into Cwm Rhiwiau, a curlew gliding songless away along the course of Nant y Cerrig Duon, which joins Afon Disgynfa at the sheepfolds by Rhyd y Cwrliwns. Leaping the stream at Cerrig Beddau, I traversed the hillside beyond and entered in. On a rock-bluff a raven had left the scapula of a lamb, paper-light, picked clean. I crossed the bracken hillside to the cairn which marks the threshold of a ritual landscape, a secret hidden behind an outcrop, and from it took my bearings to the inner sanctum of this place, where the sense of its wholeness is expressed. Under a louring sky, I scanned among reeds for the rocks, and there, slowly emerging to the attentive senses, the stone row that leads to stone circle, like birth-canal to goddess-womb, made pregnant by our reverence.

As with so many of the Welsh upland monuments, only bare and sunken stones remain to reveal their pattern to a close eye. What decoration, what sacrifice, what celebration, what ritual here? Not the faintest echo comes back to us from the bowl of the surrounding hills; we do not know; except that, for those who have gone beyond, this place has signified. As if to measure that, magically, coincidentally, synchronously as I stepped within the circle, a clearing of the clouds from the north, a shaft of sun that seeded all the rushes with diamonds. And as I walked back down that long valley, the sun itself rolled along the ridge westerly, freed of mist, and its light transfigured all, arching over me a double rainbow. I have loved this land. I have loved my woman here.

But I am by her death (which word wrongs her)
Of the first nothing, the elixir grown . . .

Above the waterfall once more, a dark dog fox loped towards
me, leapt the wall, made for the stream and turned to wade
downwater for maybe twenty yards before slipping across to
the crest of the crags and disappearing. Seconds later a pack
of baying white and motley hounds poured over the wall,
splashed straight through the water and streamed over the
hill, aimless, urgent, off the scent, Barbour-clad followers
panting after, sticks clattering, lustful to see the body torn.

But He had padded soft along the perilous ledge beneath,
and scentless now squatted on His haunches, tongue lolling,
panting, His pelt beaded with diamonds, time indistinct and
the water falling in front of Him, protective, transfiguring,
like a goddess veil.

STONE FIELDS

The Knockduff Gallán, County Cork, Ireland

Bernard O'Donoghue

The townland I grew up in was called Knockduff, 'the black hill'. And most of the land in our farm was indeed black, like Kavanagh's: eternally facing northward, towards Doon, 'the Fort', where I went to school. It was a hard farm to work, they always said, mostly climbing upward through rushy ground. It was no surprise, they said, that my father, like his father before him, died at fifty, and that energetic Mick Mac who bought the farm after my father's death also dropped dead, suddenly, even younger.

The exception to this heavy blackness were the four fields to the sunny south, to the front of the house, which were the only good land on the farm. They had more hopeful names than the black ground of the furzy glen or the coarse meadow or the guttery gap or the Inch down by the river. They were known collectively as 'The Four Fields', and individually as the Gate Field, the Stone Field, Jackson's, and the Western Field. They were where the fine hay was saved.

The Stone Field took its name from a five-foot-high standing stone at the north-western corner. The Irish word *gallán* was in general use for such stones, defined by Dinneen in his great Irish dictionary as 'a monolith, a pillar-stone, *oft.* supposed to have been thrown by giants from the hills, *oft.* bearing an ogham inscription'. We *oft.* traced with our fingers the lines and striations on the stone's sides, trying to see some

alphabetic significance in them, but I don't think it was there. Our stone had a pointed top, just below which was a cup-shaped indentation. It was noted in the various books recording the antiquities of the parish of Millstreet and the barony of Duhallow – most notably by Fr James Ferris who in the 1920s tramped through every godforsaken field in the parish, itemising everything. Of a similar stone on a farm a few hundred yards away, Fr Ferris reports the view of 'the old people' that giants threw it from Clara mountain. Ours was said to have been thrown by Fionn MacChumhaill from the beautiful, round mountain Caherbarnagh, the nearest of the Derrynasaggarts which faced the four fields across the five miles of fertile river-valley behind the village.

The stone stood about forty feet from both the northern and the western corner of the field, fifty yards north of the quarry that had been mined for building-stone or for the pencil spread as hardcore for the farmyard. The quarry had its own significance: early in the twentieth century, a young man from the neighbouring Keeffe farm was bringing a load of lime from Shrone, at the foot of the Paps, through a blizzard. Late at night his horse and car came plunging into the farmyard, driverless. Next day they found him, frozen at the bottom of the quarry which he had run to, driven mad with the pain from the lime that the wind swept into his eyes.

Both stone and quarry were a nuisance from the point of view of the efficient farmer; neither bothered my father because he laid no claim to being a good farmer. Like Denny Hickey, the collector of all local points of interest, archaeological and familial, he felt that good farmers were stronger in the arm than in the head. But when Tommy Dominic cut the hay, the tractor had to get as close as it could to the stone without hitting it with the chattering teeth of the mower-blades. The space taken by the quarry was a thousand square feet of good ground wasted. This never failed to be lamented by the hay-savers, especially in fine years like 1959 when the hay was so sweet and dry and valuable. But when the dog came wagging his tail through the gap from the Gate Field, leading in the bearers of the gallon of sugary tea, it was in the uncut canoe of grass around the stone that we gathered to rest, where the older men – Phil Micheál and Jack Sweeney and Paddy Fitz – cut their tobacco plug and drew on their curling, aluminium-lidded pipes. We had ancient, greying black-and-white photographs (I don't know where they are now) of those assemblies around the stone that stood like a *pater familias* in the middle. It was a natural place to sit; sometimes we even leant against the stone itself.

Mick Mac, who bought the farm when we sold up and left after my father died, was an excellent farmer. In his second year in the place, he bulldozed the stone into the quarry and covered it over with the small stones and earth from the long ditch that divided the Stone Field from Jackson's. So he reduced the four fields to three and created a new, big central field that had no name. The following spring, getting up in the cold early hours to help a cow calving, he dropped dead, aged 42, on his way down to the yard. He should have left the stone standing, everyone said. Like the stone, he was unfortunate to live in the short gap of time between superstition and archaeology. Before his time, no matter how much the land was prized, no one would interfere with ancient monuments, the edifices of fairies and the púca and the Fianna. After him, monuments were protected by government edict. Irrational belief and rational history were equally effective as defenders of these ancient monuments.

Forty years later, I can see where the quarry was, because the ground has sunk in as it does over a recent grave. And I can see where the ditch was between the Stone Field and Jackson's because a neat line of ragwort is growing there. Its growth is prohibited by law because it is poisonous to cattle. The Irish term for ragwort is *buachalán*, a word surviving, like *gallán*, in local usage, which has retained its malefic potency much more than the raffish English botanical term. There was another stone, also noted by Fr Ferris, lying flat in the corresponding north-west corner of the Western Field. I can still line up where it was by looking beside the ditches that thread your eye along to the handsome top of Caherbarnagh from which Fionn MacChumhaill had thrown the gallán to land upright in the corner of our field.

So I suppose we could put the stone back again if we were mad enough to want to. We could stand by it again and look south-west to the mountains through whose footlands we could see the train hooting along in front of its diesel racket which marked the Hours of our days in the meadow as regularly as the Angelus: 9.20, 11.05 and 3.10 into Millstreet station. The flat stone too now lies at the bottom of the quarry. But there wouldn't be any point in resurrecting it, because we no longer know what it meant or what it was for: why it stood at exactly the angle it did, or faced the way it did. Its potency was due to things we don't understand.

Looking at the place now, it is like the scene of an old killing. This feeling is reinforced when you see the stones that still stand in other places. Near where my sister lives, outside Bandon, there are the extraordinary four stones of Castlelack, the tallest of them a good ten feet. To reach these you have to drive up a winding road which seems repeatedly to stop in a farmyard before picking up the thread again to work its way round another upwards bend. When you finally see them, scornfully upright fifty yards from the road, you would no more think of knocking them down than of shooting an elephant. From your vantage-point next to them your vision covers all points: west towards the hills of West Cork; due south to the light that always changes over the sea; north towards the heart of the huge county, and east towards the city whose presence you can deduce from the misty glow over Cuckoo Hill.

In our townland 'the stone' referred to the gallán in the Stone Field without any possibility of confusion. And because of the dominance of the home stone in our lives and imaginations, it was inevitable that we would be drawn to places like this (Ireland is full of them) where the level horizon in all directions radiates out from these groups of monuments, aligned in a way that is clearly calculated but obscure. It is the same experience every time: you find 'Standing Stone' marked on the map and you seek it out in some unlikely place. First there is the satisfaction of finding it, and then you are taken by surprise every time by the sudden realisation that you can see unimpeded in all directions, whether you are standing on upland fertile ground, or on a mountainside, or nowhere in particular. First we tracked down the local stones: the beautifully angled, much photographed, pencil-like stone at Knocknakilla on Mushera Mountain near Millstreet, in its circle of lesser stones, pointing west like the arm of a sun-dial. Then a couple of miles further south, to the back of Mushera, you have to work harder to find a moss-covered circle of stones inside a copse of forlorn pine-trees, choking to death from light deprivation. Next to it there is a strange, abandoned 1950s house with fading acid-blue hydrangeas spindling through the broken windows into a room which has a long, improbable church pew underneath the fading inscription 'Up the IRA' in bold letters along the snocemmed wall. Green moss has wrapped itself round these like nature's anoraks. Ten miles to the west of us, just over the border in Kerry, there is a magnificent standing stone in a townland, Gallaun, which is named after it. When we went a few summers ago to see it standing in its wide, fort-like ring, the farmer on whose land it stands came out to switch off the electric fence around it, to make our approach easier. Like Ted Mullane, on whose land the Iron-Age boat lies near Millstreet, he was proud to have this majestic monument. The member of the Fianna who hurled it northwards from the Paps, our most magical, twinned mountains, must have had a stronger arm than any good farmer.

Twenty miles to the east there is the astonishing Carraig Cliona (Cliona's Rock), at Bweeng near Mallow where a man from our side of the country was bludgeoned to death with a heavy farm-implement (maybe by his father-in-law, maybe not; nobody was saying): a huge block of limestone that you lie on top of to examine the skyline. Like many of the stones in these parts, Carraig Cliona is associated with a malevolent goddess. Cliona is defeated by the clever young woman who recurs in Irish folk-stories, such as those about the Gobán

Saor, the stone-mason of the fairies. Big as Carraig Cliona is, it is not easy to find. Until you are right on top of it, nobody seems keen to acknowledge its presence. When Denny Hickey took us there, we had to abandon the map and stop at three houses to ask for directions. This always pleased Denny, who kept the conversation going until he discovered some common acquaintance.

Once you have found Cliona's huge rock, it is hard to believe that you couldn't see it for miles. The name Cliona has recently been domesticated as one of the most popular girls' names in the new Ireland with its fondness for the exoticism of Gaelic legends. In his wonderful book about folkloric wise and/or malevolent women, *The Book of the Cailleach: Stories of the Wise-Woman Healer*, Gearóid Ó Crualaioch tells the story of this most extraordinary and bulky of the presences in the Stone Fields. In fact, there are two Carraig Clionas in remote places in County Cork; the other is near the sea at Rosscarbery in the spectacular holiday-making centre of West Cork where visitors gather in increasing numbers from the European Union, amid godwits and curlews and peregrines and choughs. Down there it makes sense because Cliona was one of the three daughters of Manannan Mac Lir, the god of the sea. She was drowned by a great wave, Tóin Cliona, named after her. But Cliona's rock, down in that more beautiful setting, does not have the formidable bulk of the inland stone, hidden away among the agricultural labours of North Cork. And what on earth is this sea-goddess doing in the good farming land near Mallow, forty miles from the sea? Was this vast boulder thrown from the sea rather than from a mountain-top? It is hard to think of a suitable term for the figures of female power that gave their names to these great stones that accompanied them: the Irish word *cailleach* is usually translated as 'hag', but the witchlike overtones of this term are not appropriate. The word is too emaciated. Similarly, Robert Graves's 'White Goddess' has an ethereal air that doesn't meet their solidity. And the term 'goddess' has an air of familiarity that disenchants these remote figures.

Because there is nothing mysterious or esoteric about what

I am saying. I am describing the most solid and permanent of literal truths. You can't fail to have this feeling when you finally get to Carraig Cliona, past the ragged farmyards and rusted tractors and collapsing haybarns that surround it. The great rock of Cliona is itself a mystery; nobody knows how it got there, or who put it there, or what it means. It is also true that it will still be there, and I suppose will still be unintelligible, when we are gone. Maybe it will still be a mystery to the creatures that slowly mutate from the insects that, they say, will survive our atomic end.

Many of these great stones, it is true, are seen – and guardedly half-venerated – as survivors of another life that have stayed indissolubly in the air of our world. Like Lot's wife, you might want to say, Cliona was turned into a pillar by a figure of male virtue or authority. Several cases in Ireland represent the triumph of the Christian holy man who turned the cailleach into rock. She terrifies the people; his vengeance is to petrify her. But of course it is an ironic, Ozymandian vengeance. Her petrified form goes on dominating the landscape long after the saint's bones have been pulverised and even his stone church is falling apart: 'a broken chancel with a broken cross'.

And I suppose it is this kind of reflection that made us so shocked by the bulldozing of our stone into the quarry. But its absence, its invisibility, mean that it remains undefeated. It continues to be present to the imagination, like the chestnut tree from his childhood that Seamus Heaney talks about, as significant a presence thirty years after it was cut down as when it dominated the farmyard. If we put our stone back up, it would not be the same thing.

One of my favourite sentences in the whole of English literature comes from Sir Thomas Browne's *Hydriotaphia or Urn-Buriall*. Browne ponders the Roman sepulchral urns excavated near his surgery in Norwich, and reflects magnificently: 'Time which antiquates Antiquities, and hath an art to make dust of all things, hath yet spared these *minor* Monuments'. When I memorised it the first time I read it, I thought what so much attracted me to it was the wonderful stylistic counterpoint between the Germanic monosyllables and the orotundity of the two capitalised Latinate phrases. But thinking about it again now, I suppose the sense of the sentence was what attracted me more deeply, drawing me back to our Stone Field and the monument there that Time had spared so indestructibly. Compared with these great, impassive survivors, all our measures of time are insignificant: train-times, Angelus, early deaths, the changing seasons. The Old English elegy called *The Wanderer* puts it conclusively: 'Here money is transitory, friend is transitory, man is transitory, kinsman is transitory'.

But in the end, transitoriness is not the point. What these stones most express is the accidental nature of survival: evolution at its most perverse. Some stand in fields; some are still ringed by circles. Most, no doubt, are invisible. All are undeciphered. The strangest thing of all is that the feeling they instil in their observers is not an Ozymandian despair: 'look on my works, ye mighty, and despair'. They make you feel reconciled to the arbitrariness with which Time makes its choices. They make you think, like Thomas Browne's sepulchral urns, that everything may come round again. And that it doesn't matter anyway. We mustn't get above ourselves.

THE STILLNESS OF STONES

Presaddfed Burial Chamber, Anglesey / Ynys Môn, Wales

Tristan Hughes

They stand close by, on the edges of my attention and vision. They are a mute and static background, a piece of scenery, and my focus is on other, moving, things: an arm that wheels in front of my eyes and hurls a husk of shining red leather, hard and fast, down towards my feet. 'How is that?' will be the question. And, as often as not, the answer will be an unfurled index finger. But at least there will be an answer.

Sometimes, during these long summer Saturdays at Presaddfed, I'll sit behind the boundary rope and watch as the occasional visitor makes their way through a gate into the field opposite, maybe pausing for a second or two to glance over at the enigmatic ceremony of our game. What must they think? A group of men, all dressed in white, who stand carefully around a bunch of sticks pushed into the earth. Some of them carry wooden clubs; some of them point and shout out strange words – an outlandish liturgy, which to the uninitiated is as remote and incomprehensible as Latin. Some of them guard the sticks with a priestly vigilance, while others try to wreck them and whoop and holler when they do. But at least there will be an answer here too, spelled out in faded, peeling letters on a sign: Bodedern Cricket Club. And perhaps, in a thousand years, when that sign has crumbled away, when men play with laser beams in fields of Martian dust, when time has turned enigmas into riddles and mysteries and unfathomable rites, they will make our ground the object of their pilgrimage, and look at the holes the sticks have left behind and the shreds of white cotton and crimson leather, and they will wonder what took place here. But for now it is we who are the answered question, the background scenery, and their destination is about two hundred yards away: eight stones heaped in a field that might once have been anything at all.

Or maybe not quite anything. They say that they were built for the communal burial of the dead and call them passage graves or cromlechs, dolmens or tumuli. They say that maybe they were the sites of some fertility cult, the Stone-Age churches of an unknown creed. They say that just maybe, at a stretch, they could have acted as primitive astronomical observatories, marking the revolutions of the prehistoric sky. But beyond this there are only more maybes. The gaps between these stones are infinitely smaller than the gaps in our knowledge of them, and our guesses echo through these spaces like fragments of a conversation in a vast, empty room.

And the stones of Presaddfed leave more room than most. Few monuments could be less spectacular. Set low down in a damp field on the floor of a shallow, boggy valley, they look from a distance like a giant grey mushroom nestled beside a peaty cow pat. A closer inspection reveals them to be separated into two groups: one still upright, with four slabs holding up a thick, weighty capstone; the other, a few steps away, no more than hefty, asymmetric rubble. Unlike other sites on the island, such as Barclodiad y Gawres and Bryn Celli Ddu, they have been left naked, denuded of their cairns, with no restored covering to suggest a particular use or an original state. Even the prospect around them is meagre and limited: to the south and west gently sloping hills obscure the horizon; a rising line of woods flanks the east; while to the north you can just about make out the strange white sails of the wind farms at Cemaes. It's as though whoever chose this place to build did not want to encourage the eye to wander, to offer it another place to go.

Travelling here, I often feel as if I'm leaving the island I think I know behind me, that with each mile it is being stripped down and away. The journey is short but the alteration is startling. Moving inland from the eastern shore around Penmon and Llangoed, with its lush fields and woodlands and wide sea views, I watch as the ground and horizon appear to contract and pull back like the flesh of diseased gums, revealing pale rocky hummocks topped with sparse tufts of gorse and wind-bent blackthorns. From Llangefni to Bodffordd to Gwyndy to Penyrorsedd, it becomes ever more pared and elemental, making where you have come from seem like a green hallucination, and where you have arrived an unexpected landscape of stone – a skeleton land poking out through pinched, impoverished skin.

*   *   *

Ynys Môn is rich in stones. Some of this wealth, I admit, we islanders have never fully appreciated. I remember one of the worst jobs I ever had was helping my father pluck them out of a potato field he'd just ploughed. They were an awful crop, and froze my miserable hands as I flung them into the nearest hedgerow. And who knows what unearthed treasures I threw away those days – axe heads and flint arrows and the shards of urns, enough to make an archaeologist weep – and whether these might not have proved a great deal more valuable than the potatoes that replaced them. It was an easy mistake to make. Come down the A5, to where it goes over Telford's bridge, and you will be welcomed with our island's proudest, oldest, and most abiding boast, blazoned there in green letters: *Môn: Mam Cymru* – Anglesey: Mother of Wales. You learn the story early here, part of an Anglecentric education that tells you again and again how we mothered a whole country out of our abundant womb, how Wales itself sucked an existence out of our teat, how we fattened the Princes and how they wasted away when the English stanched the flow of our milk and honey. With all this in your ears it was easy to start thinking of where you lived as a miracle of fecundity, to imagine that just by standing on its soil the wheat and corn would begin sprouting out of your fingertips. And all the stones? Well, you could just throw them aside; somewhere out of the way, somewhere out of view.

But they've always been here. On the edge of our islanders' vision, perhaps, an obdurate incongruity in our golden dream of plenty, but also proof of the power of that dream to misdirect the focus of our gaze and have us look for riches where they no longer exist. Because others have rarely seen the island quite as we'd like to, or as we'd like them to. Take an early visitor, Giraldus Cambrensis, in 1188. His first observation is straight to the point: 'The island of Anglesey is an arid stony land, rough and unattractive in appearance'. He sees the stones first. Only then does the dream, the history, the myth, creep in behind his eyes: a few sentences later he is pointing out that 'in its natural productivity it is quite different', praising the 'richness of its soil and its abundant produce', and remarking that in 'the Welsh language it has always been called *Môn Mam Cymru*'. And Giraldus's efforts to adjust and accommodate what he has seen to what he has heard becomes almost a refrain in the accounts of the many travellers who followed him. Here, as a random sampling, is Joseph Hucks in 1795: 'Anglesey (though it is called the granary of Wales) appeared to us as one continued picture of desolation'; S. Baring Gould in 1905: 'Anglesey does not impress the visitor as being so fertile as has been supposed'; and Robert Roberts in 1923: 'in spite of the richness of the soil and the populousness of the country, there was a barrenness about its appearance which was not pleasing'. I'll whisper it here, out of the hearing of the Anglesey Tourist Board. Historically, the most common initial response of travellers to the island would seem to be disillusionment and disappointment. To an extent they have all, like Giraldus, seen the stones first.

But then again, maybe that's because it's the stones they came to see. None of them really journeyed here to witness agricultural marvels, to draw a breath of the fructifying air. They came to see monuments and remains: the castles and the churches, the menhirs and the megaliths, not the living body but the remnant bones. The touch of long-dead human hands redeems the very material that has often been taken to be a symptom or index of barrenness. And of late, it must be said, that redemption has become our salvation, because now – whatever the case may once have been – it is out of visitors' pockets, not the legendary soil, that our real harvests spring. As the past becomes the only future in sight, we've become grateful for crumbling walls and Neolithic leftovers. It's the old oyster parable again: how the speck of dirt, the irritant, turns into the pearl. And so time, ever the conjurer, has played a cunning trick and transformed these stones into our richest asset, our most precious resource, the bedrock of our economy. What a thing is Môn today! Fertile in graves, affluent in ruins, splendid in stones.

*   *   *

The search for redemption can take the most peculiar forms and routes. My weekly journeys to Presaddfed during the summer are not long, about half an hour by car. Others have come much further, and for reasons at once more urgent and exotic and forlorn. In 1802 the Reverend John Skinner travelled here all the way from Camerton in Somerset, where he was rector. Like many other gentlemen of the time, a disproportionate number of whom seemed to be parsons, he came to Môn in pursuit of ancient relics. These antiquarian visitors were in the vanguard of a kind of homespun and haphazard renaissance, a recovery of the misty past and civilization of the ancient Britons. And by the time John Skinner disembarked on these shores to search for cromlechs and coins and any other archaic object that might come his way, this group already possessed their own venerable place in the stock of national caricature. As early as 1628 John Earle had provided a sketch in his satire, *Micro-cosmographie*:

He is a man strangely thrifty of Time past, and an enemy indeed to his Maw, whence he fetches out many things when they are now all rotten and stinking. He is one that hath that unnatural disease to bee enamour'd of old age and wrinkles, and loves all things (as Dutchmen doe Cheese) the better for being mouldy and worme-eaten . . . A great admirer is he of the rust of old Monuments . . . He will goe you forty miles to see a Saint's Well or a ruined Abbey . . .

How many of these men were conscious of such a rift between their self-image as the embattled saviours and custodians of the British past and the popular characterisation of them as fetishists of dust and decay, as necrolaters, as quaint lunatics, it's hard to say. In Skinner's case it can safely be assumed that if he was aware of it then it wasn't something to which he was happily inured. Five days into his tour, on a cold, wet afternoon near the village of Llanfihangel yn Nhywyn, he notes: 'On enquiring at a cottage near this spot whether there were any carnedds or cromlechs to be seen we exposed ourselves to the ridicule of two old women who enjoyed a hearty laugh at our walking in the rain to hunt after stones'. In many ways this brief episode represents a variant of one of the classic motifs of the travel account: the comical disparity between the perceptions of tourist and local – the one seeing monuments while the other sees stones. Yet, in the wider context of Skinner's life, this episode resonates far more deeply, and the laughter of those two old women echoes across it all.

Skinner's account of his tour through Môn was only a brief portion of his life's great work, a rambling and eccentric *magnum opus* of ninety-eight manuscript volumes deposited in three sealed iron chests in the British Library, with the express wish that they remain unopened for at least sixty years. They chart his abstruse and often bizarre speculations on British antiquity – his pet theory was that Camerton was in fact the Camulodunum of Tacitus – and his equally odd etymological discoveries. He claimed to have found a secret significance 'in every letter that entered into the composition of Celtic names'. But more than anything, what they record is his growing disaffection with a world and a milieu which he felt neither understood nor appreciated him, and in which he, in turn, found himself bitterly out of place. They tell the story of the early death of his wife and daughter, of his endless frustrations with parishioners who regarded him with almost as much scorn as he did them, and finally of his estrangement from his remaining children, who ended up mocking the one part of his existence in which he felt at home: the world of antiquities. The more one hears it, the crueller the laughter becomes.

Posterity, to which he consigned his researches, hoping they would be vindicated, has more or less forgotten him. But he found a peculiar habitation in a wonderfully acute portrait in Virginia Woolf's second series of *The Common Reader*. There she sketches a figure hopelessly at odds with his era, the reactionary nay-sayer of a nascent modernity: 'Behind him lay order and discipline and all the virtues of the heroic past, but directly he left his study he was faced with drunkenness and immorality . . . with the overthrow of all that was decent and established and right' – a man who sublimated his despair with the present into a passion for the detritus of the past, and searched there for refuge.

All of this is writ small in his account of his tour. The island (as it ever does) disappoints him; he has never been 'in so dark and dismal a place'. And as he approaches Bodedern it just gets worse: 'it did not possess us much in its favour'. He spends an awful night in an inn there, with terrible food and atrocious lodgings. The owners prove to be surly and venal and unhelpful. Then finally, with much relief, he gets to Presaddfed. He makes a careful sketch of its eight stones, notes their positions, glances into the shadow beneath the capstone, and makes one last remark: 'Under this cromlech we were informed a whole family who had been ejected from their habitation sought shelter during the last winter'. And whenever I look at this place I wonder if the Reverend Skinner ever came to realise his affiliation with this unnamed and unfortunate family – that in journeying here he also sought a shelter of sorts in its stones, a redemptive purpose and quest to set over against his sad and troubled life. I think of him lowering his eyes into the granite murk of a tomb, seeking a solace that would ever elude him in a grey thought in a grey shade.

In 1838 he walked into a beech wood near his home in Camerton and shot himself dead.

*   *   *

You can hear the gunshots coming from the woods. They burst out in erratic clusters, and somewhere out of sight discs of clay shatter in the air. All through the summer the old Presaddfed estate resounds with them, and over on the cricket pitch we joke about it; 'after bowling that you need shooting' is a favourite. And yet, over by the stones, no more than two hundred yards away, they seem less audible. In fact everything seems less audible.

I don't know why this is. Perhaps it's a topographical quirk. Perhaps the low, marshy field in which they stand sucks in the sounds, or the surround of shallow hills muffles them. Maybe the woods act as silencers. But, whatever the reason, there's no doubt that an eerie quietness pervades this place. At first you notice it as an absence of human noise. Cars pass by as if on air, the cricketers' shouts appear to founder in their mouths. But then you begin to realise how it affects the animals too: swallows wheel about in mute circles, stray pheasants keep their beaks firmly shut, even the nervous bleating of the sheep seems to evaporate before it reaches your ears, until finally it dawns on you that this quietness and stillness is ubiquitous. The breezes that blow always and everywhere on this side of the island are often indiscernible here. You look at the wind farms in the distance and the spinning of their sails appears mechanical, separate, unreal, like snow falling in an ornamental globe. Or the inverse of this: that you are somehow trapped inside its glass, looking soundlessly out at the living, moving world.

Perhaps this is an enchantment – some revenant magic

accessed down the centuries in the shape of a dubious Celticism, New-Age spirituality or eco-consciousness. Around these silent megaliths clusters an ever-growing circle of noisy questioners and listeners, eagerly waiting on their every withheld breath. Or tire of waiting. I have heard these stones described as the 'petrified voices of our ancestors', and people have always wanted them to speak, to answer their most urgent questions. And straining their ears (or extending their hands or dowsing rods) towards them, they have sometimes heard whatever it was they most wanted, or needed, to hear.

*   *   *

In the early evening, when the game is over and all the cricketers and visitors have gone, the cromlechs of Presaddfed revert to what, for most of the time, they have really become: a home for the sheep with whom they share the field. These sheep know for certain what they are – somewhere to hide from the sun and the rain – and you'll often find them hunkered down beneath the capstones, casting a wary eye in your direction, chewing on a piece of lichen. Their residence here appears to be well established, and two deeply worn tracks mark the frequency of their visits, as well as the sheen of lanolin that coats the inner surfaces of the stones.

These graves are lived in, as they briefly were in Skinner's day. I can't help thinking that this is something the original builders would have approved of. Because they are little more, and certainly nothing less, than emblems of occupation: embodied graffiti that once said 'I am here' and now just 'I was'. They stand on the cusp of a psychological watershed, attesting to a need that their Neolithic makers did not share with their nomadic, Mesolithic predecessors – a need to settle and make one place their own, to create a testament to that belonging, turning an island into a home.

But just as this island has ever been ambiguous, a place of reversals and transformations, so it seems we have come full circle and reached back and forward to a point both before and beyond these gravesmiths. Because surely it is the wandering peoples of the Mesolithic who are now the tutelary ancestors of the modern world, and it is their restless to-ing and fro-ing that foreshadows us, not the sedentary yearnings of the tribes who built Presaddfed. And maybe that's why so many of the visitors to stones such as these have been those who are most dissatisfied and disaffected with that world – those who seek an imagined haven from its agitations and confusions and relentless accelerations, and in doing so express a submerged and vestigial trace of their own Neolithic inheritance, the living element of these relics that they carry inside themselves: a dimly remembered instinct to stand still.

Platform Cairn, Brenig, Denbighshire, Wales

Andrew McNeillie

The stonier places have always appealed to me more than the lush and cultivated. I am a wilderness man at heart, a man for Hugh MacDiarmid's 'stony limits'. Why this should be I'm not sure. What is it puts the bias or cast, the lodestone on our lives so that, given our heads, we always tend one particular way, by immediate preference? Right now, if I was at liberty (not that I'm ever at liberty), I would get into the car and head for the mountains, to find a remote black-hearted cwm I'll not name here, or a desolate piece of water on the moor. Or I'd have a stretch of wild coast in mind, followed ideally by a chastening, brisk trawler-voyage to a small rocky island in the Atlantic. William Hazlitt called the natural world 'the last refuge of the misanthropist'. But I'm also a sociable person, a word man, happy to halt the stranger and pass the time of day on the wild road, or to prop the bar with you in Aberstyx, to hear the story of your life, the troubles of your heart, the joys and sorrows of the world. No one is simply one thing or another. And isn't that part of the fascination of stones? They seem to be one thing, nothing but what they are, and for ever.

I say that I'm a materialist, but not, you understand, in any grasping sense, except as to grasping reality. I love the very granulation of stones, the life in them and light, just as I love the life in words. I love the unaccommodating wilderness too.

Perhaps it is that from very early on, apprenticed at the age of ten to the art of fly-fishing for trout in the remotest cwms and streams of eastern Snowdonia, I learned to be self-sufficient, happier in hardship and durance, in the long vacancy of the mountain day, rain or shine, and cold: rain and cold being the greater part of it, in among the rocks and falling streams, Sunday after Sunday from 1 March to 30 September. I would be in the company of three grown men who, making no concessions to my minority, expected me to get on with it, through thick and thin. They had their minds on higher things. 'No man is born an artist nor an angler', Izaak Walton said. I must serve my time. I must perform my tea-boy duties too, making a fire of heather stalks and waftage, in among the rocks, though the airless granite rain be perpendicular, or the wind set fast in the east, on a poor day, day-without-end as it would often seem, world-without-end, up where the kettle takes an age to boil. Amen.

Was it a surrogate religion we pursued, out in the wilderness, and a religious habit or devotion I acquired there at the stony limits? I don't think so. What temptation did we ever resist up there? The only temptation we knew was to cry off and not go in the first place, on a cold wet morning with the wind in the driving seat. Unless it was to resort to the worm, as only Trevor did? What was our god but the brown trout? The sin-full dark-hearted Bible was in my world in those days, no doubt (much doubt), but not on the home front (for a mercy). Yet a Scottish Presbyterian mindset surely underwrote our denial, as did the Calvinistic-Methodist emphases in that good old Welsh schooling I endured of sure foundation. I knew about guilt. I knew about the wilderness and about the stones of the field; that man shall not live by bread alone and that angels shall 'bear thee up, lest at any time thou dash thy foot against a stone'. (I hadn't heard of Dr Johnson then, on his tour of the stormy Hebrides, and how he proved the existence of external reality by kicking a stone – and not an angel to be seen, but fallen James Boswell.) When at the age of nineteen I went on a pilgrimage to Inis Mór (the poet Yeats's 'most desolate stony place'), I at once thought it chastening and paradisal. So before long I would return to live all but a year there, among 'the stony lockers . . . on Aran', as Dylan Thomas called them in his poem 'I, in my intricate image'.

Stones in their intricate image are what they are because they weather, in two senses. They wear and resist, withstanding whatever's thrown at them, and have done for aeons, while the sands of time run on. They are all metaphor and none. They may be impermanent like the stars themselves but they are so on a timescale that only serves to emphasise how brief and fleeting our lives are. They remind us of our vanity. We are like glancing stonechats or wheatears on an island summer day, momentary birds in passage, beside the deciduous Atlantic. Hence we have headstones and tombstones, urns and mausoleums *in memoriam*, dust to dust, for brief gravitas and gravity. For naked we came into this world, naked as stones, and naked we leave it, in unsure and uncertain hope of we know not what. But I have my suspicions.

Despite the Old Testament warning that 'Thou shalt not remove thy neighbour's landmark', and against all current principles of conservation, I have on my window sill a small cairn, a minilith, of rocks and stones, pocketed from four locations (Wales, Scotland, Ireland, and America's Walden Pond). I often contemplate them and stare into them when, as now, in mid-sentence, lost for words to write. They stare back. They

>   . . . hold their cold
> ovals and angles steadily, rock steady.
> Lodestones to my uprootedness they
> anchor me, weigh me up and down, all told,
> though I leave out of mind the place
> I took them from, for charm and talisman,
> for that burden's too full a refrain
> ever to be my saving grace.
> Mornings I cover them with outspread
> hands and feel them numb to the bone,
> as if I reached for them in a streambed.

> They're as cold, god knows, as ice,
> like the gaze of one who has
> the measure of you and all you ever said.

They give 'no answer' which, as Ted Hughes put it, is also an answer, like a refrain. That word 'burden' is an interesting word to bear down on here. For it also has a singing, Biblical sense, by which it rises up, against gravity. Stones make light of their burden. The Bible speaks somewhere of 'lively stones'. I cannot dwell on stones without sensing this paradoxical or metaphorical thing about them. Here the Welsh or 'Silurist' poet Henry Vaughan casts a rational, yet a religious, a theological, shadow on proceedings, in the dedicatory poem to his 1650 volume *Silex Scintillans* (sparkling rock):

> If the Sun rise on rocks, is't right,
> To call it their inherent light?

Is there no light 'inherent' in the human soul? But especially on a bleak upland day, Vaughan notwithstanding, stones seem to me to be composed of light, rather than being star-like catch-all mirrors or mere matter. They flame and smoulder everlasting in forty shades of grey, brighter than any burning bush. They are the beacons in the wilderness, if anywhere in our archipelago is wilderness. If anywhere is remote anymore.

Perhaps the early morning is the nearest most of us ever come to remoteness now, and silence. Some places in the wilds might be hard of access, like the route not taken on a rockface: but see how the climbers are queuing up to try, down there where the scree fans out its skirt, a crick in their necks, an itch in their hearts to dice with death, remote not remotely a word in their vocabulary. A curse on all their houses, I'm tempted to cry, voice echoing out across the stony air of the cwm, like the bleat of a sheep. But we mustn't bleat, nor must we mystify. People like to say that the past is always close at hand in a Welsh landscape. But the past is remote everywhere and always, remote as yesterday. We cannot communicate with the past and only sometimes with each other. History is a smokescreen to a mystery. It burns like gorse in spring, to encourage new growth.

When I came to this task, this little word-labour among the stones, words from stones the devil's commission, I had first in my mind's eye the image of a dolmen I would set out to discover. It stood away beyond a wilderness of bog and heather. It grinned at me like a gap-toothed crone at the hearth or threshold of her summer's ruined *hafod*. Or with its bony arse bared to the sky, a cloud of skirts hoiked up behind, I'd catch it pissing through its stony wishbone into the face of winter on a wild and windswept day, the half-door of history hanging all but unhinged behind it, and the rain without end, world without end. That was the way I used to see Maggie Feaney on Inis Mór, in her black skirts and shawl, thirty years ago and more, when the Atlantic gale was up so high it might blow her away as soon as look at her, a witch on a broomstick, down the side of her cabin for a pee. How the broom blows.

But I came in the end to Brenig, on my native heath, on the moors of Clwyd and Dinbych, the Denbigh moors, hard by Mynydd Hiraethog (mountain of longing or loneliness), half mindful and smiling as I thought that in my unreconstructed youth 'Denbigh' was synonymous with 'the loony bin'. There the poet manqué Leonard Brookes, now no longer of this world, who taught me English Literature, had periodically to go when life and stony-hearted boys and girls got too much for him to bear, or so it was believed, when suddenly he wasn't there, and absent said the unofficial register, poignantly, for weeks on end. (Let this be his muse's memorial.) How easily the mind's delicate balance tips, and topples all to nightmare, in our glorious western infirmary.

Like the line in Hamlet, my own unaccommodated spirit haunts 'north-northwest' of where for now I'm doomed to make my home. So strongly does it haunt that when times are hard and work relentless I tend to crave the wilderness to distraction. That way madness lies, as King Lear says, out on the crazy, bareforked heath, at the ineradicable limits of allegiance. (Poor Tom's a-cold.) For sure, Dinbych's moors, like any others, are inhospitable, even to sheep. None the less they still catch at my heart with their bleak skylines and I shall never forget drifting on long runs down Llyn Brenig, as if to eternity, hearing the local anglers calling to one another in Welsh, 'Welsh things . . . as from the edge of home' in Ivor Gurney's poem, through the failing evening, the trout rising, elusively, explosively. World without end. But it's true the moor is inhospitable for so much of the year that the remnant hardly adds up to more than so many memorable fishing trips or a couple of picnics on a summer afternoon. Unless you are native *and* local, instressed into the inscape and *cynefin* of the place. Otherwise, for the deracinated, it's all a snapshot outing, however often repeated, when the curlew might or might not deign to cry its sorrow to an unforgiving world, or the basking adder, dreaming of Eden, startle and beat a hurried retreat as the kettle on the primus stove (first among equals) hissed itself awake, now so long ago, labouring to boil even at that elevation.

I will not mention afforestation's contribution to the heath's desolation. I won't deplore the chainsaw massacres of ripped trunks and blasted battlefield trenches, the machine's heaped carnage: fate to come to the alien conifer legions that are now halted up there on the ridge, poised as if to reconnoitre their fate, or crowded down by the lake, like beasts penned at an abattoir, for the briefest shelter from modernity's storm and holocaust. This new lake that was once, and on my 1947 map remains, mere Afon Brenig, and Afon Fechan, peat streams in the bog, wild with primrose-bellied trout, adrift under hag or boulder, rising to the midge, full as a mare in foal, to tickle your fancy. And when was that? I have forgotten. (I disremember.) A year after I first drew breath. Then twenty and some more before they drowned out their chatter and blinded them to the freaks of upland light to regulate the Dee (the 'Cambrian readjustments far upstream' of Geoffrey Hill's *Scenes from Comus*), to slake how many thirsts? The thirst for knowledge, that begs all the questions.

Experience has taught me that the best day for a thing is the wrong day, for anyone who would learn from experience, that is. And it was the wrong day when I came back to Brenig. No sooner was the sun up than it removed all shadow of doubt, not a cloud in the sky to hint of rain, and the fish stayed down, while the fishermen reached for their sun-block. For the other thing that made it the wrong day, the wrong week, was the international fly-fishing championship. There was a flurry of film crews at the tourist centre. Officials came and went, full of unfamiliar purpose. Loud hailers shepherded contestants to the official photograph. It was like a darts match alfresco, but without the consolation of beer. It was the wrong day. Put it down to experience. Draw a line under it.

Besides, I do not like to plan for pleasure. How can you? I prefer to mull and dream over a map under Baudelaire's bright lamp than to use one to find my way. I would rather beat about the bush, be lost-and-found and late reaching my destination, for the best things happen out of the way, unlooked for, in pockets of space where distance is time. Just so, I've always liked the gnomic mode. 'An eagle is said to know the place where it can find its prey, but not the time', wrote Giraldus Cambrensis; 'A raven knows the time, but not the place.' Like the eagle, I came back quite early next morning, to the wilder northern limits of the lake, before anyone else, any *living* soul, I mean, had set foot and (as the man said) set forth. Daybreak it was not, for daybreak as I've said is remote, as the raven knows, if he knows nothing else. Blink and you miss it. But it was early enough to know it for what it had been once (how the bloom fades), cool dawnlight on the water, the wind briefly unsettled, unsure of its intentions, waves lapping on the spot, and dew on the moorland road, like the leavings of a light shower of rain. On the buffeting air black-headed gulls shrilled as they mobbed a raiding crow, as they would all day, incessantly watchful for their young's welfare, their first broods, and the safety of their new clutches, on the little lake isle where a pair of black-backed gulls stood on a hillock, biding their time, up to no good; and a solitary oyster-catcher piped a single liquid pipe as it swooped to land, between two sheep on a slope of nibbled pasture. Then not one but three ravens, like an omen, rose on the wind from the ridge above, and honked and cronked, and wheeled away, perhaps from the carcase of a lamb in the heather. While the water slopped and slapped and flapped and flurried by the shore, incessantly, as it would all day, for three-and-a-quarter miles, the length of the *llyn*.

It is at this end of the water that early man beat us all to the worm of fate. Whoever he was or his wife, before the flood. It was to visit one of their cairns, somewhere to the east, on the hill, that I had come to make my pilgrimage, unsure as yet whether it would prove to be fit enough subject or destination for this essay.

A stretch of water the length and breadth of Brenig breathes light and air into the day, and glare and magic, and shadow and detail on a grand scale. It is like a waking dream of dazzling minutiae to walk along a moorland shore, by a sea of heather and moss, and in July of starry canna or bog-cotton, in no hurry to be anywhere else. But you need to settle into it, to acclimatise on re-entry to the earth's inscape and simple atmosphere. Even one unusually gifted in the art of wilderness haunting and general mooching, such as I am (I take no credit for it), must take time to find his feet again, if he is to make good his escape (oh good!), in the wake of wage-slavery, at the manic vortex that is postmodern, globally-networked, so-called life . . . (O rail your heart out against the world.) It is like riding a bike. You don't *forget* how to idle. You don't lose your balance and fall off though you wobble a bit at the outset, as capitalism's time-keeper tries to hold on to the key to your body-clock and wag your psyche's pendulum to death. So I pottered round, orientating myself like a lost soul, the wind about my ears helping to hold eye to object by muffling the world with a tide of sound, the very noisy stuff of silence.

The artists at the tourist centre had made their stab at it, modelling and painting, in a gloomy little grotto, members of a Bronze-Age tribe (according to what likeness – 1970s native Welsh? – if you forget the unlikely garb, the trim beards, the bared female breasts, the apparent social harmony). Or were they the Mesolithic hunter-gatherers who once dwelt where I now stood? Here were the signs they left behind them, so long ago, now not far from the water, a burial mound and a ring cairn. I wandered round them and between them, noting a pinkish moss in the fine grasses on the mound, a bleached and barely identifiable Marlboro pack degrading, and, as elsewhere, the fine white flowers of heath bedstraw, a few marsh thistles and nettles, a tongue of ladder fern. The stones that made the cairn's ring had patches of iron rust in them, among the rough medallions of lichen that blotched and badged them. They were all furred texture and mottled light and lithography. The moor today is not a stony place and if the terrain then bore any resemblance to it, the tribe must have gone to some trouble to find their stones. But what resemblance could it have borne? How very much less even than the 1947 Ordnance Survey bears to that for 2003? Let me send you home to think again.

The site here, invaded and plundered, was not an especially atmospheric one. It did not keep me long. And soon I set off down the shore, avoiding the unmade road. This steadily led me astray, happily out of my way. The cosseting but bright and sparkling water and the soporific siren light and air within the heather bogland seemed to lull and lure me on. I was held on course as if by a current at the meeting of two waters, where a windrow forms, between heather and lake. On the opposite shore the day before I had seen sand martins dart at certain-death collision speed into their nests under the eroded bank, where miniature bays were formed by the attrition of the waves. Peat martins I thought to call them, for their backs are peatbog brown. What brake horsepower they have. But there weren't any to be seen this morning as I stepped along, up and down, here and there among the heather hags, across the mossy holes and hollows, down to where the feeder stream runs in, a remnant tributary of Afon Fechan, I suppose.

I came up past a low fir below the track where sheep were grazing in the morning shadows, between the tree and a drystone wall, and the tree was alive with a busy constellation, a host of pied wagtails pursuing flies – a new brood I suppose, or more than one, fluttering in the wind, beside the lake. Then I must go on uphill beyond the track, with not even a sheep-path to follow as the heather grew more rampant. Now looking back down at the lake I could see a flotilla of boats advancing north on their outboards as the fishermen renewed their competition. The higher I climbed and the more distant and Lilliputian the several clusters of boats became, the more they reminded me of the fleet in Galway Bay on a sharp day all that time ago and however many miles away. The wind was too strong and the small boats ran hard against their drogues among the breaking waves and had to keep peeling off to start a new drift, sooner no doubt than the fishermen would have liked. So hard did it blow that one boat was driven broadside on against the rocks and couldn't be relaunched. The fishermen struggled, wallowing and stumbling, but they were no match for the wind. I climbed on up beside a sheep fence in which the pales were so old they were completely furred with grey lichen and looked as if they were made of nothing else, and no longer capable of supporting but supported by the rusted single strands of heavy sheep-wire. Then on at last to the little plain of desolate eastward heath where the ruins of Hen Ddinbych (Old Denbigh), a medieval farmstead, or perhaps a hamlet, still mark out the ground and beat their own bounds in the bleak moor very clearly.

The 'platform cairn' when finally you find it, high on the hill above Hen Ddinbych, is startling to discover, and exactly the place to choose for such an excursion as this, though the cairn might have been nothing and sent me about my business to find another somewhere else. (It was a task maybe for my summer holiday. For I have a second heath, a world elsewhere, beyond Wales, north-northwest again, where my roots also reach and hold me. Perhaps Galloway's 'Cairn MacNeile' itself might rise to the occasion?) But this one seemed to rise beneath my feet. Bread from stones is a wilderness story about temptation resisted. These stones, in their great circle, were like petrified loaves, stones from bread, long or round, the whole baker's dozen of shapes, scarce an angle or edge to be found, as if shaped and hefted for handling. They form now a broken cobbled floor, several yards in diameter. At their westerly lip they stand a foot and more, eighteen inches perhaps, from the earth, neatly built round and curbed and coped. They tempted me to walk across them, to rest on them and take stock. Like Robinson Crusoe on his island I gazed out upon the shipwrecked world. To the east was all dreary heath, with patches of grazing. And breathing down my neck now, to the north-east, stood the Roman legion of gloomy firs, vainly camouflaged in plaid of pyramidal pattern of imbricated dark and lighter green. I could hear them, whispering to each other to be quiet or they would be seen. Then to the west and below was the *llyn*, a cheap interloper it suddenly seemed to me, like a five-minute wonder compared to the stones on which my hands rested, stones that had been so skilfully placed there by other hands, how long ago, at what bidding, on what principles, by what co-ordinates, in what unsure, uncertain hope, to entomb what corpses, in what name? No answer is also an answer. But I looked up and, the horizon being clear twenty or thirty miles away, and sparklingly sunlit, I found one that is surely irrefutable. The best and most enduring answer you could have. For the view from the cairn takes in at a glance the whole panorama of Snowdonia (and the Berwyns too), north to south, half an inch to an inch high to the naked eye, with the peak of Tryfan, that rises stark 2000 feet from the floor of the Ogwen valley, near dead centre in the picture. There is surely no more startling vantage point from which to gaze upon those ancient, igneous stony limits: a skyline, from start to finish, that hasn't changed since the world began, where, as Hugh MacDiarmid put it, 'all is lithogenesis'. Whatever else the folk knew who built the cairn, they knew that, I'd say. But had they ever been there, stood at the precipitous peak of Tryfan, stood beside those two great standing stones they didn't know as 'Adam and Eve', and looked this way? Or even, risking life and limb, did they hop from one to the other, as breathtakingly blasé mountaineers nowadays do? What was the range of their territory? What did this vision of the mountains mean to them, 'bright visible but coming and going with the weather' as Gerard Manley Hopkins said of it, from a poorer vantage, near St Beuno's? No answer. Though Hopkins would not agree. Nor probably would they. But the rest is words words words. The rest is smoke from burning gorse. The rest is silence and has the measure of you and all you ever said.

In a Bright Blue Mist

Y Fuwch a'r Llo / The Cow and Calf Standing Stones, Pendam Mountain, Ceredigion, Wales

Niall Griffiths

WINTER

No snow up here, but unthawed frost, thick enough to be snow, crusts the tops of the two stones like icing and sticks to the fronds of lichen on their flanks like ghosts of those growths, like their shadow-negatives, like vegetation from ice. The larger stone is circled by a worn groove in the iron-hard ground where people of a certain bent have walked deasil around it. The smaller of the pair, the *llo*, is dotted around by molehills as if the soil itself rises in attempted imitation. The two pillars themselves appear to echo the huge humps that swell behind them and to each side. The anterior slope was once thick with fir but is now bare; the cash-crop has been reaped. It is freezing up here; the thin air crackles with incipient ice. Breath can be seen and can be felt hardening into a scab around each nostril. There is no sound, apart from your own respiration; breezeless and birdless, the stones and the mountains and the molehills remain pushed up into what seems dead air. As if nothing will grow or move up here ever again.

❊   ❊   ❊

This is what I heard:

That in mid-December 1917 he returned home on a week's furlough from France and the war. His face was white and sunken and his hair was greying, and although he bore no physical scars the ever-wetness of his eyes and the rattle of his cup against the saucer in his hand as he took tea with his family spoke of another kind of trauma. That first evening, after tea, he drank beer with his father and ate *cawl* around the table and his parents and sister sought to make it all welcoming and comfortable for him and so asked him no questions concerning the fighting, even though such queries boiled within them. Words did not seem to sit easily within him; he had to coax and cajole them out one by one at protracted intervals, as if he were re-learning a past skill now corroded with disuse. After tea they sat in front of the fire and he smoked a cigar. He went to bed early as the snow began to fall again outside, fresh flakes sticking to the snow that over the past few days had hardened into crusted ruts around the cottage and in the lane. After banking up the fire, his family also retired, the three of them moving silently between kitchen and bathroom and bedrooms, avoiding eye contact, drifting mutely as if in deference to his uncharacteristic taciturnity. Water splished out of taps and feet shuffled on the rugs and candleflames threw their elongated shadows up the whitewashed walls. Beds creaked and groaned as bodies settled in them and the snow went on falling outside.

The plummet in temperature woke them two hours later. They came back to consciousness with chattering teeth and faces numbed. The father and mother got shivering out of bed and met the daughter on the landing, from where they could see the wide-open front door and the upright rectangle of night it exposed like a standing grave, large flakes of snow falling through it in shallow zigzags. Wordlessly they dressed, several layers each, hats and gloves and boots and shawls and scarves and oilskins and greatcoats, and the father lit a storm lantern and they stepped outside and followed the footprints in the snow along the lane and up the hill, further up the hill towards the lakes and the forests, the prints gradually becoming less discernible as they were filled with fresh snow. The lantern swung in front of them and illuminated nothing but darkness slashed by snowflakes and the whitening ground underfoot; no stars shone above and their laboured breathing was the only noticeable sound until, almost at the top of the mountain, just before the tree-line, they heard the first screams. Wordless screams, unspellable, like nothing any of them had ever heard before, not even from the abattoirs within earshot of the cottage. A man's voice unleashing shrieks and bellows of horror and rage and disgust somewhere beyond the trees, in the vicinity of the lakes, repeated screeches of disbelieving grief slicing through the icy darkness.

They ran towards the noises. The lantern bounced before them and made the tiny section of the world it illuminated seem shredded and battered and exploded – smithereened trees around them and the snow-covered ground and then the lakes like fields of ice and the moon in them like a drowned god – and still the screaming went on, over and over, louder as they neared it. How could one throat produce such sounds? How could one breast brew such clamour? They ran past one lake and skirted another and did not see the white owl rise like a freed soul from the ice-speared grass behind them and they ran through trees, on to where the mountain top opened out into unsheltering moorland signposted by the two ancient megaliths, and the screaming there was louder than anything they had ever heard and they stopped. The lantern's yellow light caught the son and brother with his arms wrapped around the larger of the two stones and his left cheek pressed against it so hard that freeze-dried blood cemented his face to the old cold rock, his eyes looking at his family but not seeing them, looking through them at something that was drawing those sounds from his mouth, those terrible screams which went on and showed no signs of cessation as all three members of his family attempted unsuccessfully to lever the frozen, clutching fingers away from the rock.

SPRING

Still some bite to the air up here. This far from the sea and this early in the morning, frost remains, carving ghost-ferns onto the stone and into the runnelled mud in which the stones are set. A sunbeam strikes the quartz in the hill behind the megaliths and promises warmer hours to come, illuminating the dew on the cobweb that links the two stones, a delicate umbilicus that attaches the cow to its calf. The maker of that bejewelled thread hangs equidistant between – small, fat-bodied spider awaiting whatever prey this strange and still and lofted world might offer. The cow-stone has a vertical groove running down it, reminiscent of a vagina – perhaps the birth canal from which the calf-stone emerged or was hewn. In this recess, a thin scrim of ice has melted so water now drips and trickles down to the molehilled and sheep-shitted earth below. The sheep that left such spoor have been moved to lower, warmer pastures in preparation for lambing. Transhumance has gone on around these stones for millennia; a million spiders have slung their trapezes between them, several thousand springs have passed, and if their silent witness means anything we think we can understand then we haven't understood anything at all.

*   *   *

This is what I heard:

He was the son of a psychiatrist and, as is often the way with such people, massively ill-equipped to exist happily in mainstream society. In the garden of the house where he spent his childhood lay a mound of moss-furred grey boulders once arranged into the shape of a cottage in which, several centuries ago, a child was born who became a legendary poet. A plaque, inset into the garden wall, commemorates his birth and life and death in a few terse sentences in three languages. People of many nationalities go there in pilgrimage and curiosity, and some of the son's earliest memories are of playing amongst the boulders, searching for insects or lizards or small mammals and being observed by a string of faces peering at him over the garden wall, faces of many different shades of skin colour, all quiet, all inquisitive, all seeming to study just him and his innocent endeavours. He moved out of this, his parents', house in his late teens but moved back a few years later; there he remained for some years, slowly curling into himself and slowly letting the world shrink around him, losing all interest in the procession of faces that came to gawp over the garden wall. Then he left the house again in the middle of an April night and took with him some utensils and a sleeping bag and some spare clothes and no money and he let the mountain guide him with its contours up and further up, away from the boulders and the faces and the confining gravitational draw of the valley floor, up towards the forests and the lakes and the megaliths and the moors and the sky which at that moment of his setting out sparkled with steering stars and blessed him with a benevolent moon. He moved up towards that bright satellite until he felt that he was closer to it than he was to the busy human world below.

For a while he vanished. Few concerned voices were raised at his disappearance; the police did not exert themselves – he was not a criminal. But there were those who looked for him, took out beseeching advertisements in the local papers, posted signs to lamp-posts and phoneboxes, informed various missing persons bureaux and trekked across hills and through forests calling his name, all with no response. And then, after a month or two, talk began to circulate in the local towns and villages of odd apparitions seen on the mountain; hikers and outdoor-partyers and paragliders and fishermen began to swap stories about a form seen leaping through the trees or silhouetted on the peaks – a figure of a man, his face obscured by wild and matted hair, dressed, it seemed, in filthy sheepskins and rags and bedecked with necklaces of bones and teeth which they all imagined clanking, even though they were out of earshot. On occasion, he could be heard chanting or singing somewhere in the woods; peculiar peals of idiopathic laughter drifted down as the yeti capered, long-limbed, and gibbered over the mountain's flanks. On one occasion he was seen by a drunk couple as they took the unpoliced back road home from a pub, standing on one of the peaks, erect like a cairn, howling at the moon like a wolf with both arms outspread like a sacrifice.

And then the corpses began to appear, around the two standing stones. Throat-cut and disembowelled lambs placed carefully on top of each megalith with their loose heads dangling so that the blood seeped into the rock; broken-necked rabbits laid before and between the two stones. Crows tied with twine spread-winged to their sides as if in mid-flight collision. And once a fox strung up between the stones, swaying in the thin air, its brush an inch off the earth and its soundless snarl offered to the sky. This went on for some time; complaints to the police and rangers escalated, so eventually they came up the mountain, armed men among them, and found him in one of the shallow caves, stinking and cowering and dressed in uncured sheepskin seething with maggots and a thousand cuts scabbed over on his skin and his eyes as wild as the wind. And they took him down off the mountain and away from the lakes and the trees and the moors and the megaliths and back down to the houses and the roads and the streetlights. I was told he didn't want to go. I heard they had to sedate him to get him off the mountain.

SUMMER

A rare sight, this; some predator-bird, probably a merlin, has used the *llo* as a plucking-block. This usually occurs in more remote areas, but evidently the raptor's hunger has driven it to risk the road and its traffic, scarce though that may be up here, on this mountain pass. Black and white feathers identify the carcass as a pied wagtail, but very little remains; one foot with the toes clenched like the legs of a dead spider, an eyeless head with the tiny yellow beak agape, some dismantled bones and a static flurry of feathers, blood-nubbed. The merlin's mutes dot the stone in a series of scattered flat coins like another species of lichen, and the smaller bird's blood has dried to a few black streaks zipping the blue granite. This is summer's herald; the change from cold sterility to warm abundance is declared in this small carnage. The trees from which both predator and prey appeared and the indifferent provision of the stone remain unaltered by the earlier dawn.

*   *   *

This is what I heard:

They picked her up in Llangurig after she'd walked the six miles or so from Llanidloes. She: hitching to Aberystwyth from the outskirts of Birmingham to visit a close friend at the university. They: a middle-aged couple in a lilac Volkswagen with a dreamcatcher hanging from the rear-view mirror, returning home from a rave on the banks of Llyn Brianne. They originated from the midlands of England too, from Smethwick, but they'd lived in mid-Wales for a couple of decades. Her gratitude for the lift made her tolerate the condescension evident in their declarations that they couldn't comprehend how she could choose to live in such an awful place when she could live here, as they did. She told them she didn't want to move away from her young son or distance him from his father, however estranged she herself might be from him. The woman said something to the man in pidgin Welsh which made him snort with laughter. The hitcher indulged them, as she did when they diverted out of Ponterwyd and up onto Pendam mountain – the scenic route, as they called it. Her patience held when they parked the car next to two standing stones, one smaller than the other, and continued to hold as they got out of the car to link hands around the taller stone. Though invited, she did not join them. She watched them from the car as they embraced the stone with their eyes closed, saw the hawk circle them as if in curiosity and then wheel away on a flick of sickle wings as if in quick dismissal. She listened to them chant, observed them as they held the stones in turn and murmured indiscernible entreaties into the rock. Watched as they stood back a metre or so from the stones and then leaned forwards until their palms were supporting their body weight and remained like that for almost thirty minutes as the blue sky began to contuse above them and shadows stained the hills around. When they eventually got back in the car her patience had waned and she was relieved to be dropped off in Aberystwyth on the promenade outside her friend's halls of residence and glad when the couple wished her luck and drove off. The sun was setting in a furnace of red over the sea.

That was two years ago. She has forgotten what they looked like and how they sounded, but she has a recollection of a smirking mouth and of the sound of snorted laughter, of amusement expressed nasally. But the stones – she still sees those in dreams, while Birmingham blares outside the bedroom window. She could describe them intricately, although she has never laid eyes on them since that first encounter. She finds herself discerning their likeness in sand on a beach, in her rumpled bedspread, in mashed potato on a plate, even in the humps and bulges of her own body and that of her infant son and his father from whom she is no longer estranged.

AUTUMN

There are rents and gouges in the mizzle-softened earth at the base of the stones where badgers have been digging for slugs and grubs and roots in preparation for the coming cold. As if a small earth-mover has been at work here, or a gang of men with picks and trowels, these deep slashes in the soil have a kind of urgent savagery about them as if the animals that have made them know of the severe and unforgiving nature of what awaits – that harsh and lethal force that has already stiffened the grass round about and turned into friable dullness the deep green that was the dominant colour up here only yesterday. Circling the base of the stones, these hackings at and in the earth suggest that something has been trying to uproot the megaliths, to undermine them. A portion of the larger stone, not seen for some years, has been exposed and claw-scratched; it looks moist and mud-stained, more like purulent flesh than granite, now to be rained on and shone on and blown on. It is as if the stone has grown a little, overnight, as if a few inches' sprouting from the mountain has augmented its height. As if one thing up here will continue to live and move in the coming months when the ice re-appears and the badgers are burrowed deep in the earth, within a slumbering mountain.

*   *   *

This is what I saw:

We are driving home over the mountain, my brother and my girlfriend and I, from a pub on the other side of the massif. It is past midnight and summer has gone and the air up here has sharpened again and our headlights are the only point of illumination on the mountain-top except for the few stars and moon that appear intermittently through the drifting clouds. White moths flutter across the bonnet and burst and break themselves on the grill and windscreen and we are hoping to see a fox or a badger or an owl maybe, but all we see is sheep. Our faces and necks and arms are midge-bitten and inflamed because we sat outside for our first few drinks by the river, and now we scratch ourselves, worrying away at the tiny but maddening pink welts the minute insects inflicted as they took our blood. And then, as we drive and gaze and scratch, we catch a quick glimpse, between two rocky humps ahead of us that are darker than the night-time sky, of a bright and luminous blue, a kind of opaque ultramarine light which we drive into as we round a corner. Lit by something neither headlight nor moon, we park the car and stand in silent awe, staring agog at the thin blue glowing mist that has settled in the dips and troughs of the mountain-top like some kind of liquid. I don't know why it glows so, or why it appears so blue, but it is one of the most beautiful and breathtaking things I have ever seen; it is as if the earth around us is still forming in fire and in ice, still slowly writhing as geological powers twist it into shapes and formations, releasing vapours from fissures and shafts, the greasy by-products of the smithy that works within it. Either that, or we are witnessing the final collapse, and are standing amid the end's exhaust.

We climb a small mound so that we may see more of the mist and assess its extent. It has settled in the hollows so humps appear to rise above it like islands in a sea. I have lost my bearings somewhat as the mist has defamiliarised this landscape, but from my vantage point I realise I can see the stones, or their top sections, truncated by the blue mist at their feet. They seem like beacons in an ocean, buoys, closer than I thought, twin solidities in a fluid shifting mass, offering anchorage in surrounding uncertainty, and it seems to me as if the mountain itself has generated this mist, a blue covering for its face, almost like a veil of shame or mourning for what, over the aeons, it has witnessed of human passage. Yet the stones remain visible, unmasked; monuments just to guide and amaze, that's what survives of us up here. If this mist is suggestive of a final conflagration engulfing the world below, then what will remain of us are monuments designed to guide and astonish.

I stood on that mound for some time, between my partner and my brother. We stood on the mountain for quite some time, lit by that bright blue mist. Then we got back in the car and headed off the hill for home, and I did not look out of the window at the megaliths as we passed by them, within a few feet of their flanks, because they'd still be there tomorrow.

THE POETRY OF STONE

Pentre Ifan Burial Chamber, Pembrokeshire, Wales

Gillian Clarke

Stones, hauled from the mountain, set upright, steadied and rammed tight into the ground to bear the great weight of the capstone. Seen from below, across the fields against the sky, the cromlech is an awesome sight, yet familiar. We know it as we know the letters of the alphabet. It has become the very sign for the word 'stone'.

But it is not just stone. It is, somehow, sacred, in the same spirit as the little Celtic church at Mwnt, or the Cathedral at St Davids. It is the human mark on it and the human arrangement of the stones that catch our breath. It is the fact that, against the odds, human beings went to such lengths and endured such hardship to bring vast blocks down from the mountain to build this tomb. In the fourth millennium BC, a group of Neolithic people was moved to collaborate on the mighty work of raising one of our earliest public monuments. They settled the slope at the western end of the Preseli mountains to cultivate crops and keep their animals. Yet food and shelter were not enough. Above them, the stones of Carn Meini, an outcrop on the hill, stood ready for quarrying. It is fine granite, hard igneous rock. Ancient upheavals hurled molten stone from deep in the mantle of the earth. All sedimentary rock, formed later, has eroded away, leaving the hardest to jut in giant slabs against the sky.

*   *   *

Beside me on the table are three fragments of planet Earth: a granite set – igneous white stone speckled black and winking with quartz; a small block of purple slate from Penrhyn – five-hundred-million-year-old metamorphic rock marked by nothing but the slate-man's tools and the ice that split it as neatly as a book falling open at the page you were reading; and a tablet of limestone about three hundred million years old – a photograph of a moment in the life of the warm shallows of the littoral before the seas withdrew and left it high and dry somewhere in what is now Derbyshire. The limestone is cut and polished, teeming with sea lilies, a stilled seethe of primitive life-forms and shell fragments, and what looks like one very small trilobite as real and wide awake as if it lived. It is like footage of old Movietone.

If I set two of the stones on end and place the other on top, they make a cromlech. Close to my desk, leaning against bookshelves, is a life-size limestone hare, sculpted by Meic Watts, its polished body another moment frozen from the life of an ancient sea, 'a premonition of stone' from the Palaeozoic.

> In its limbs lies the story of the earth,
> the living ocean, then the slow birth
> of limestone from the long trajectories
> of starfish, feather-stars, crinoids and crushed shells
> that fill with calcite, harden, wait for the quarryman,
> the timed explosion and the sculptor's hand.

I've returned again and again to the poetry of stone. In 'The Sundial', one of my earliest published poems, I see not only stone but megalith as I watch my young son 'calculating/ the mathematics of sunshine'. From the simple observation of a child making a sundial out of a circle of paper and marking the hours with twelve pebbles, the language of poetry found the parallel. The child, like the primitive man in the Neolithic, is finding his way in a world with no maps; the mud-pie, the sandcastle, the pebble and driftwood house are how a child learns all over again what early man discovered – that these materials are for human use, art, and imagination. Out of the stuff of the earth we can make pots and axe-heads, dens, cathedrals, a sundial to calculate the hours of the day and seasons of the year, a telescope to observe the stars. Years ago in Samarkand I was shown the forerunner of the telescope, part of a ruined fifteenth-century observatory. The sextant was a tunnel of stone slanting from earth to sky, revealing, square by square, the map of the stars as the earth turned in space. In the Boyne Valley in Ireland, the famous passage grave of Newgrange shows that its Stone-Age builders needed to know exactly when the shortest day occurred, to calculate and mark it precisely. They used a beam of sunlight. At dawn at the winter solstice the rising sun sends a ray of light through a slit in the portal to touch the wall of the chamber. On no other day of the year can that happen. Newgrange, Stonehenge, and the observatory in Uzbekistan are milestones on the road to our understanding of mathematics.

*   *   *

The granite set, the oldest of my three samples, the enduring material that has made some of our most impressive megaliths, comes from Pembrokeshire. It was cut to pave a city courtyard or street, 'a floor hewn from the batholith'. Monuments made from limestone have been badly worn away by time and weather. They loll in their circles like melting snowmen. The granite ones seem untouched by time. No wonder the rock was prized.

My three rocks tell Earth's story. They mark time from nothing to inert stone then to early life and all that the word 'life' promised – and threatened. Abraham, Jesus, Mohammed. Dante, Mozart, Hitler. My children. Their children, one of whom is named Ifan. The spotted woodpecker at the bird feeder, now, and the now-ness of that flight of lapwings over the fields. Their small cries.

*   *   *

Igneous, metamorphic, sedimentary rock. How I loved my *Guide to Minerals, Rocks and Fossils*. I loved its language, the names of rock. Earth took its time with it. It took ages. Then life began, fidgeting and wriggling for an unimaginably long, slow time – for ages, aeons, chrons. It is natural to be drawn to stone. It is human to stoop and pick up a pebble glowing among all the others on the beach, then another, more beautiful than the first. Soon pockets are full and one must choose the best example of the red, the rust-gold, the green. There's a pure white one, a smooth grey with speckles or a ridged band of quartz, a veined blue. They can't all be carried away. At home in my room I spent hours sorting stones into spirals and rows according to colour and size, counting, grading, arranging them on every available surface. Ga, my grandmother, in Fforest Farm, Pembrokeshire, never minded my pebbles. Back in south Wales my mother was more house-proud. '*You* don't have to dust!' she complained. '*You* don't have to dust!' I'd reply.

Dust. Ashes to ashes, dust to dust. Water washes stone away. It didn't wash me away. There was no sign that my skin was any the less for the hours I spent in the sea. That was the mystery. Rock, even granite, turns to dust in the wind and the rivers. Stones are sucked and licked and turned by the sea until they are shingle, then sand, grit, sediment. The sediment settles, lies flat or slumps into the sea and turns again to stone. Waves have spent all of time making pebbles, their salt tongues hollowing caves, undermining cliffs. Could I suck a pebble until it dissolved like a sweet? Would there be, at the very last moment, a seed, as in an aniseed ball? What would you grow from the seed in a stone? I knew, as a child, that crystals grew, that they accrued, multiplied and made themselves in the dark. The seed of a stone is a grain of sand, millions laid down, hardening again to make sedimentary rock which will, in turn, in the lick of wind and water wear away, ground into sand again. And so on and on reshaping the world, its bumps and hollows, its soils, allowing each plant to evolve in a particular locality, thriving on nutrients and conditions apt to its needs. You can taste rock in spring water, in wine, in a beetroot pulled from the earth and simmered till its skin just peels away. The wine expert Jancis Robinson writes of the taste of wet stones in Chablis, and flint in Pouilly-Fumé and Sancerre. 'A Local Water' came from sipping spring water:

> Under the hill
> water runs in the dark.
> Rains that have spent history
> seeping page by page
> through the strata,
>
> run black in the deep aquifers
> to rise bringing its gift,
> the formula like a spell,
> a gulp of cold that silvers
> at the touch of light.
>
> *Calcium, Magnesium, Potassium, Sodium,*
> *Chloride, Sulphate, Nitrate, Iron.*
>
> Sip this, the poetry of stone,
> a mineral Latin in our blood, our bone.

*   *   *

The igneous tuffs and granites of the Preseli hills – the oldest rocks in Dyfed, their craggy shapes against the sky above sloping fields – are characteristic of the landscape of Pembrokeshire. Carn Meini, thrown from the earth as it was forming thousands of millions of years ago, and Pentre Ifan between them mark moments in the making of the planet and in the story of early humankind. I knew that Carn Meini, from which Pentre Ifan's granite came, was the source of the inner circle of 'bluestones' at Stonehenge. But what were 'bluestones'? And why did the builders of Stonehenge think them so special that they bore them so far by sea around the coast to the Bristol Channel, up the Severn estuary to the Avon, and up-river to Salisbury Plain? Yet bluestones aren't mentioned in my *Guide to Minerals, Rocks and Fossils*. Archaeologists and geologists don't talk the same language, and neither explains the term. Carn Meini granite, a mixture of rhyolite and a spotted dolerite with a slightly blue colour (at last, somewhere, I found it described as 'blue') made excellent polished stone axes which we know Neolithic people used. Axes made from Carn Meini stone have been found at megalithic sites in Ireland. To the seafarers of the Stone Age on the crossing to and from Ireland, Carn Meini must have been the first and the last sight of Wales. It was both landmark and lure, as it was to me as a child in my father's car driving to the coast, looking out for the first glimpse of the sea.

*   *   *

I passed no childhood day without the company of stones, without a pebble in my pocket, without using the sea-smoothed boulders of a beach as stepping stones to the sea, or playing in sand, or trudging through shingle, or leaning against the sun-warmed rocking stone on the cliff at Fforest to read, draw, and write my diary, or picnicking at a megalith. The port of Barry, close to where we lived in south Wales, was bombed during the Second World War. Once I was old enough – say, four years old – my father took me to Fforest to stay with Ga. Often, one or more of my father's three sisters were there too. My mother, pregnant, already with my young sister to care for, chose to risk the bombs to be at home in Barry with electricity, a proper bathroom and a hospital close by. Later they all came for a few weeks in summer, but I would not be persuaded to go home with them. When the war ended, and I started school, we went to Fforest for all our holidays.

Here myth intervenes. First a personal one. It must be a memory made of layers of experience, story, snapshot, hearsay and imagination, images laid down one on the other like sedimentary rock: a picnic with my father at Pentre Ifan, playing close to the cromlech and seeing the blue sea through its huge windows. It was like a church, its stone roof balanced like a feather on its pillars, each window the wind's eye. The oldest roof in Wales, the oldest building, yet not so holy you had to whisper, not too sacred for cheese sandwiches and *bara brith* spread with Ga's salty home-churned butter and a bag of windfall apples and a flask of sweet tea.

The sea as seen from Pentre Ifan is a distant blue line, a ribbon of Cardigan Bay beyond the sands of Newport and the black shingle of Fforest and numerous other little coves and bays a few miles away. It is difficult to date that first visit to Pentre Ifan. Why do I not remember the temporary structure of oak beams raised to hold it steady during the archaeological excavations conducted by W. F. Grimes and his team? Have I erased the wounded stones and replaced them with the cromlech as I later encountered it? Or have I confused a picnic at the cromlech with a picnic at another megalith, the rocking-stone at Fforest? Grimes had the oak structure erected in 1937 to support the monument ready for excavation of the ground close to the portal. The work was interrupted by the outbreak of war in 1939, and the strengthening beams were left in place for over a decade. I was a baby, a small child, a schoolgirl during that time. Ga died in 1944, and after her death it was into the care and company of my aunts and uncle that my father delivered me every school holiday. To make a memory of that picnic at the cromlech, maybe I have remembered Pentre Ifan unbandaged from its war wounds sometime in the 1950s, standing whole against the sky and sea. To accompany it, I must have summoned my grandmother from an earlier time, shaking a feather mattress at an open window, pegging white sheets on a line. That picnic scene contains elements that cannot have existed together. The rocking stone, or logan stone, balanced on the south cliff at Fforest is the more likely site, just a walk away from the house down to the shore and along the beach, across the river, along a muddy path through woods, and out on the open track that went firm and dry up the cliff between bracken to the headland, the perfect place for a picnic. We'd sit on dry, sheep-cropped grass, lean against the warm stone, eat our bread and cheese and watch the sea. We looked for the head of a seal, or a ship on the horizon. Here a public myth sails in from Ireland. We take possession of it. It is my father's gift to me, stolen from the *Mabinogion* and its traditional associations. Now it is ours. A ship might be one of Bendigeidfran's, returning from Ireland after the tragic mission to rescue Branwen. According to my father, the rocking stone against which we lolled was a pebble from Bendigeidfran's pocket, and one day he would come to claim it. With any luck I'd be there when it happened. In imagination, in family mythology, and perhaps in megalithic history, Pentre Ifan and the rocking stone at Fforest are connected.

Years later, when I returned to the cliff at Fforest, there was no stone.

> On the headland is an absence
> where it fell some winter night
> between here and childhood,
> and the sea's still fizzing
> over a bruise that will not heal.

I swam out into the bay to the headland and dived. The waters of Pembrokeshire are clear as glass. Did I find the giant's stone?

> Do I see it through green translucent water,
> shadow of a wreck, a drowned man's shoulder,
> a clavicle huge as a ship's keel
> wedged between rocks?

Is this how we make myth, and make sense of the world? Pentre Ifan was a place of wonder to me. I remember, from more visits than I can count between childhood and now, the mystery of how the megalith is grounded, a great weight on the earth, yet how the vast capstone seems scarcely to touch the uprights. You can see light pass almost all the way between orthostats and capstone. You'd swear a piece of paper could slide between them. It makes light of gravity. This is a place where stone has been hacked from the mountain, handled and hauled and hoisted, showing how already, in the Stone Age, we were architects, inventing, working together to make what archaeologists have called a public building. The orthostats have been chosen with care. The two portal stones match and curve to echo each other. This is no crude, basic building. It is design. Long ago, men chose these stones, brought them from the mountain, lifted them into place, stood back, saw what we see now, and were satisfied. In 1624, in a work entitled *Elements of Architecture*, Sir Henry Wotton wrote:

> In architecture as in all the operative arts, the end must direct the operation. The end is to build well. Well building hath three conditions. Commodity, firmness, and delight.

Pentre Ifan is indeed commodious enough to contain mountain and sky, the distant sea, six thousand years of stories and all the mythology a father could pass to a child. It is the very epitome of firmness, originating as it does from the earth itself, and holding for so long its rootedness upon it. And delight? It is the one, perfect design for a cromlech. High enough for a horse and rider to pass beneath it, as an early illustration shows. Other cromlechs are squat as toadstools in comparison. Pictogram. Portal. The elegant initial letter in a book of stone.

Note on Poems Quoted

Page 67, ' a premonition of stone' and 'In its limbs lies the story of the earth': 'The Stone Hare', from 'The Stone Poems', *Making the Beds for the Dead* (Carcanet, 2004).

Page 67, 'The Sundial', from *Collected Poems* (Carcanet, 1997).

Page 68, 'a floor hewn from the batholith': 'Granite', from 'The Stone Poems', *Making the Beds for the Dead*.

Page 70, 'A Local Water': uncollected poem, 2005.

Page 73, 'On the headland is an absence': 'Rocking Stone', from the title sequence of *The King of Britain's Daughter* (Carcanet, 1993).

Page 73, 'Do I see it through green translucent water': from poem 14 of the title sequence of *The King of Britain's Daughter*.

STATIONS

Stone Row, Parc y Meirw / The Field of the Dead, Llanllawer, Pembrokeshire, Wales

---

Damian Walford Davies

There are no beelines to stones. The digressions have to matter.

Thundering through Dinas Cross on the outside of the Mail-coach a century and a half ago, miserable men, hunkered down in greatcoats, roused themselves to doff their hats to the Lady Stone, leaning alluringly at the side of the road. The custom warmed them. Sodden Victorian millinery was only the latest in a long line of ritual compliments stretching back four thousand years. She's visible through a gap in the hedge, and someone devotedly cuts the grass to within inches of her hem every week in summer, but few motorists along the A487 acknowledge her now as they accelerate south towards Fishguard, or shift down into Dinas. I always offer an awkward salutation. But friends with her, fond of her, as I am, today she's not my quarry. She's a daylight, wayside presence, a public stone; the stones I'm tracking inhabit grimmer ground. I indicate left, inland, towards Llanllawer and the megalith sentinels of Parc y Meirw: The Field of the Dead.

To haunt stones is to be familiar with these turnings-aside. I enter a different space – tumescent, overflowing, late June's hedgerows encroaching shamelessly on the lane. Nippled Mynydd Dinas – known to aroused nineteenth-century topographers as The Maiden's Breast – offers a cairn-strewn contrast to the green profusion around. On maps, the summit appears as Garn Fawr; on local lips, it's Garn Fadog, the name of the nearby farm, impossibly white in this weather. A little further on, somewhere down one of those lackadaisical tracks, rambling Fagwreinon sells honey, honeycomb and beeswax; it's closed today. In passing-places, a sense of accumulated patience. The white *Business Express* van passes so close I can smell the driver's cigarette as he coolly waves his thanks. His stereo plays the latest from The Killers.

This is the high ground above glaciated Cwm Gwaun, that dissident, green republic that jealously keeps a different calendar. Each bend up here is stone blind. Then the gentle descent into sparse, lost Llanllawer. The church of the iron hand, or church of the fox. No sign, no village, just a scattering of disparate dwellings and the sad profile of St David's Church, ruthlessly exposed in its raised, circular graveyard.

Over a decade I've watched it decline. The two Dark-Age cross-slabs in the gateposts may have been proof against malevolent intruders, but proved useless against the assaults of the secular westerlies. The churchyard has invaded the interior, ivy creeping through the unlovely tracery of Bath stone to root among cracked, haphazard tiles. A small organ, at an angle, occupies the middle of the nave; the pews are gone. Outside, the grass is knee-high; I follow in the aftermath of a recent visitor round the shell. Both decay and superabundance. Near the path, another contrast, incised in stone: Maria Llewelyn, died 1890, aged 26, 'from Fagwreinon in this parish' – the sweet farm I've just passed – and next to her, her father Thomas, buried 1894, aged 80. Her epitaph trumpets the flower of her youth; his, with a verse from Job, the 'shock of corn in season' of his age. Swifts cut the air above the bunkered cowl of the nearby holy well, to which people repaired with both blessings and curses. Inside there's a mineral dampness despite the heat; it smells seasidy, of rockpools. Tied to the gate by those who still wish in wells are frayed lime and yellow ribbons, two feathers, a posy, a necklace of silver stars, a sticker proclaiming flower-power. Even well-dressing moves with the times. A few coppers spangle the moss floor. All blessings?

Wayside stone, church, well: all stations in my cautious orbit of the megaliths, which are beginning to exert their gravitational pull. This is a return journey. I've been to the stones before, with someone who refuses to return. He's not a person you'd describe as hypersensitive. Something isn't straight there, he says, despite the stones' alignment. Nothing to do with the inevitable folk tales of the spectral White Lady who is supposed to worry the place. Rather, an invasive, very real, sense of disorder and dislocation. The junction near the well, half a mile west of the field, is as far as he'll come. He's not alone in this. I've heard that some people still take the circuitous route over the mountain, adding a good twenty minutes to their journey home, to avoid passing the place. Regular people. I don't know.

So at this crossroads, I can already sense them, gauge I'm in line with them. Heading for the high hay fields near Dinas, a tractor labours past, pulling a grotesque raker, its articulated shafts, rotary frames and long, sprung barbs retracted like the legs of an injured spider. A Land Rover approaches down the flank of the mountain, grinding into low gear as it rounds the last bend and sees me manoeuvring inelegantly out of the green shade of the layby. We coincide at the junction, where the driver scans me from his elevated seat. My safely urban, mudless Punto looks pitifully prim next to his no-nonsense box of a vehicle. There's a moment when we realise we've delayed too long simply to pass each other without at least some words. Perhaps he thinks I need directions.

So we get talking. There we are: engines switched off, two abreast under the Maiden's Breast, blocking the lane for a good forty minutes. His window remains wound down only half way.

He owns the nearby fields, and sets me straight. It's his neighbour who farms the Field of the Dead, which, properly, is the field adjacent to the one over which the stones preside. He refers to the latter as Parc y Cerrig Mowr, The Field of the

Great Stones, or Parc y Pyst, The Field of the Stoneposts. He
suspects, though, that fairly recently they were farmed as one.
Been here forty years; hasn't felt anything bad in there
himself, in either field; wouldn't know about *that*. Of course,
he's familiar with the stories. Would like to see the Ladi Wen,
one of these days . . . Some talk of a battle hereabouts: turned
up something in two inches of topsoil some years back. All
sorts come to the stones. Have I seen them?

The conversation turns, somehow, to real estate, house
prices, the young chap from Carmarthen who's just bought
the church for a song and is going to do it up and live among
the graves and sing to himself each Sunday morning. One
man replacing a congregation. I picture him drawing his
curtains, early, to read of the Llewelyns, late of this parish.
Two girls on horseback, one wearing a bikini, ride in and out
of my rear-view mirror down towards the bridge at
Llanychaer, our rural gridlock clearly striking them as
curious. No other traffic. At intervals, the farmer shouts over
his shoulder at a restive, unseen dog. I wrest the conversation
back to the troubled tenancies of the fields. Again, he
wouldn't know about *that*, but there was this acquaintance
from over the mountain . . . a character, a bit funny. He knew
about water and drainage, field contours, the mechanics of it,
that sort of thing. Came one day a few years back to help
bore for water, access a spring, in one of the fields near Parc y
Pyst. There he was, going deeper and deeper into the clay,
when he pulled up and told the lads to move towards the gate
at once. There are dead men down here is how he put it.

He smiles. I ask him whether he believes such divination.
He barks at the dog again. Not really, he says.

He's been glancing at his rear-view throughout our
conversation, as though anticipating something from the
direction of the stones. We see the 4x4 at the same moment.
In no apparent hurry, he tells me about the gentry house on
his land – 1812, five-bay, stucco – which some agent from
London recently took a shine to, then raises his hand to the
driver of the jeep and moves off downhill. The Vitara follows
him. For a moment I'm left again in one of those concentrated

pools of heat and stillness whose signature is seared June earth, brash vegetation on the cusp of decadence, and diesel.

From Llanllawer's stations, you ascend to the stones. The narrow road up the southern flank of the mountain, lined with oak, ash and thorn, red campion and stiff foxgloves, is the last stage of the approach. Gates secured with orange cord – reminders of the offerings at the well – allow momentary vistas into the fields that decline sharply into the valley to the south. It's a disorientating drive: only half a mile, but each bend an uncanny simulacrum of the last, with the journey disturbingly amplified, the stones unnervingly deferred. I knew about the battle – the 1081 clash of Welsh kings known to history as Mynydd Carn. Adrift from co-ordinates, the name echoes suggestively, elusively, in the annals. But this was the place: the scree and pastureland tumbling down from the cairn on the crest, and the great declivity of Clyn-gath beyond, the killing ground of Mynydd Carn.

The same bend, the stones thrown into the future again, and you've passed them, missed them. There's a sense of being thwarted by them. I reverse the car into the field's angled entrance. That feeling of residual movement after a long drive is instantly grounded by the stones' stasis. Then, after a moment of acclimatisation which they seem to share, they become silently vital, energetically stationary.

Appropriated two centuries ago to mark out the field, they stand in a hedgebank crackling with gorse. Four massive stones have not broken rank – survivors of an original alignment of eight, extending a hundred-and-thirty feet along the slope. The largest two act as gateposts, the massive, ten-foot eastern stone tied to a wooden fencepost with barbed wire. The third upright tapers to a point in a stony allusion to Garn Fawr, its backdrop; further down, the fourth gracefully inclines west. Two other stones lie encased like colossal lozenges in the hedge, one visible from the road, the other from inside the field. The remaining two are buried alive in the bank. Patched with delicate fans of grey, cream and lime-blue lichen, they have absorbed the sun all summer and are warm. But these are lunar stones, a sightline erected west-

north-west, they say, to track the minor moonset out across
the bay beyond Leinster. Nightstones, moonwatchers. Other
accounts reverse their polarity, claiming they're pitched uphill
with a ritual focus east-south-east, somewhere near the farm
of Trellwyn-fach. The stones keep us in the dark.

A sea of light sweeps down the great field to a blackthorn
hedge dividing Parc y Pyst from its sister cemetery. From the
vantage point of the gatestones, the panorama takes in the
curve of Cardigan Bay, the fanning field-systems around, and
the dense slopes of the Gwaun. Fishguard, unfeasibly close,
flickers in the heat; a window glints from Goodwick, and
goes out. The superferry is clearing the harbour breakwater,
heading for Ireland in line, just for a moment, with the stones.
Above, jetstreams west mark journeys into the past's Pacific
time, silver lines decaying into ragged tail-end vapour
dispersing into cloud. From here, the church looks whole
again.

Fresh tracks silverside the grass along the dock-leaved
boundary as far as the fourth stone. No other incursion into
the pristine park. An insurrection of buttercups. I take in the
stones along different axes, venturing out in vagrant trails to
the middle of the field and down to the border with the Field
of the Dead to get a purchase on the line. The field teems with
small, exotic lives seen only in recumbent summers.

Multiply the megaliths: imagine the grey phalanx before
the enclosure of the field, eight stones casting their rotating
shadows on open, fenceless ground. This is how those two
hosts must have encountered them towards evening in 1081
as they converged on this spot from the south and west after
what the chronicle says was a long day's march. For these
men too, they were old beyond imagining – a sinister third
cohort in the field, marshalled, ranked, rising.

What made the contending kings – the dispossessed, half-
Irish dragon Gruffudd, and Trahaearn, the old usurper –
gravitate to this place with their Welsh, Irish, Norse and
Norman alignments? Some tribal sense that this was proper
ground, that the stones might serve as audience to an
encounter that would re-map Wales by settling old dynastic

scores, personal hatreds? Did local contingents, picked up from straggling settlements towards the end of the march, have anything to say about the megaliths? It was evening when Gruffudd, who had joined hands that morning with Rhys ap Tewdwr over the bones of David in the cathedral at Mynyw, reached the plateau on which Trahaearn and the kings of Gwent and Powys had already pitched camp. The stones must have had some bearing.

The telephone poles in the field opposite form a parallel alignment. Their wires are taut with talk.

The source insists the fighting was pitiless. And the great daysleepers unmoved as the crude struggle was played out near them, among them, *chwys y llavur a'r gvaet, the sweat of the action and the blood running in streams; the anarchy of horses; Trahaearn on the ground, stabbed in the bowels, groping blindly for his weapon, his teeth gnawing the fresh herbs.* A car passes, heading up the mountain towards the cattle grid where the road exhausts itself and a track ekes a way over to Mynydd Melyn. *And Gwcharki the Irishman butchered him like a pig, and there fell around him in that place twenty-five of his guard and more in the vanguard.* The ferry blurs on a white horizon.

Many thousands. Lady Fern, Hart's Tongue, Moonwort, Christ's Spear. *And he, Gruffudd, according to his custom, pursued the fugitives with his troop throughout that night by moonlight through the coverts and gorges, the marshy ground and mountains, and throughout the following day,* while the megaliths obeyed their own chain of command, transmitting the convergence of stone line and lunar light to those who had long lost the ability to read such language.

The unfallen saw themselves reflected in the uprights, the wounded in the leaning stone. They must have buried the fallen here, in sight of the megaliths; carried the flower, perhaps, down to the simple, enclosed acres at Llanllawer and Llanychaer, washed them in the river at Cilrhedyn, or at the well, if the spring was running. Its waters heal sore eyes. Eight great faceted headstones, uninscribed, for the day's dead, and Wales realigned along Gruffudd's axis. *Let us now spell out his pedigree in relation to God. Gruffudd was son of Cynan, son of Adam, son of God.*

Near the gate, three bars, full network coverage again: the new transmissions intersecting with the old, signals from unseen stations boosting the frequencies of the stones. The car radiates heat.

The nearest turning place is four fieldlengths up. Driving back into the sun round the same bend, the same bend, visor down, looking too hard, I miss the stones again, catching the tallest only in the rear-view. The riders are at the junction, resting the horses. Hats off, they wave me past, into the black-green subway of trees leading down to Tre-llan wood and the bridge. They may be about to head up in the direction of the stones, past the gates with orange twine, seeing, marvellously, over the hedges, elevated cavalierly above their day, passing on a level with the tallest stone with its rein of spiteful wire, the horses' necks doing the work, up to the moorland beyond.

On the way down, they'll be leaning back all the way.

In two adjacent fields on the ridge off right, they may see two quad bikes performing the choreography of the season – synchronised, and very fast.

Note: The text quoted on pages 83 to 84 is the twelfth-century *Historia Gruffud vab Kenan.*

STONES IN SEVENTEEN FRAMES

Arthur's Stone / Maen Ceti Burial Chamber, Gower, Wales

Menna Elfyn

Arthur's Stone. Or should I say Maen Ceti?

*   *   *

It is midsummer and my ninety-one-year-old father seems pleased that I am taking him on a day trip to Gower. I have another mission in mind. We have all day and all day is what we will make of it. We set the clock to measure the miles, and all the while he sits and muses on the chapels we pass. *Wedi cau* is his mantra – all closed, all done in, or else the meeting houses he used to preach in have been transformed into smart abodes, all solaria and decking. All change, or so it seems, until we glide by Cefn Bryn, where gorse, heather and wild horses still claim the common.

*   *   *

Thanks to the ice-cream van nearby, the landmark of Arthur's Stone is distinct. My father sits in the car, cone in hand. I walk up to the tomb, thinking with Todorov of stone as 'a pulpit without a sermon or moral', of the moor as an 'open-air church full of the air of expectancy'. Should I stay, keep vigil, make a one-night-stand of the stone?

*   *   *

The Venerable John Williams to the antiquarian Edward Lhuyd: 'The common people call it Arthur's Stone, by a lift of vulgar imagination attributing it to a hero of extravagant size and strength'.

*   *   *

I return to the car. We don't talk about what it was I came to see. It is sufficient for my father to have seen the sea, and collect from its blueness his own surge of memories. He has little interest in oddball, out-in-the-cold quoits. Or in my lifts of vulgar imagination. For him, worship needs a place, a sanctuary, one that is water-tight. I remember our family having to retire down the long chapel aisle after the service so that the congregation could descant on whether or not the fabric of the Manse needed a new roof, whether the walls were really as damp as my mother insisted. To be a minister's daughter meant one was well versed in the ways of stones and absolutes.

*   *   *

We all recall deep play with stones. In the shelter at the bottom of the schoolyard in Ynysmeudwy I would erect them as stand-ins for a couch, a bed, a table. Our childhoods are Stone Ages. The primal urge to be close to this, the most basic of raw material, never leaves us. How luxurious the furniture seemed to me, as we held our burial of a dead bird with dog rose.

*   *   *

During Gower student days, I would go without sleep to go on the pull. I'd crouch in ditches, watching car lights go by before attempting, with others, to remove English road signs from this part of the world. An act of lifting. I'd always taken the Gower for granted. It would be our escape route from Cwm Tawe, full in those days of alcam and tin and noise. One overnight guest at our house couldn't sleep, insisting there were people clashing buckets outside all night. It didn't help that we also lived next door to the local pop works. Gower was different. It seemed clean. We were always aware that it was a different part of Wales.

*   *   *

We lived in a bilingual village, Welsh and English, double-decked in your mouth. Gower told us we were out of place. Here they had stones in their mouths. Wallicana (there's a mouthful), the Gower Welshry, was our route that midsummer day to the stone: Gorseinon, Tre-gŵyr, Penclawdd, Llanrhidian. Had we gone the other way through Mumbles (there's a mouthful) we would have been following the Anglicana road. Is Arthur's Stone neutral, beyond any difference?

*   *   *

Maen llwyth, Maen Ceti – A load of stone, Arthur's Stone: an old Welsh proverb identifying all stone loads with this Gower conglomeration.

*   *   *

By the way: in Welsh, stone can be female.

*   *   *

Conspirato is what was needed to raise that twenty-five-ton enigma of a capstone. The company of others to breathe together, to conspire. A tug of stones. That lift of common imagination.

*   *   *

Every visit to this great static place has its own dynamic. Early on a crisp autumn day I return to Maen Ceti. I can see it already has company. A figure places a child against the grain of the stone, as if trying to measure its height. A matter-of-fact affair, but also a special kind of ceremony. Searching out what small and large mean.

* * *

My companion has noticed another square stone set in the tired grass. It's a memorial to Mary Ludkin, *née* McCarthy, inscribed *CARRIAD 1935–1995*. Two 'r's where there should be one, as if affirming the inability of language to communicate just what we mean, the imperfection of living. There's a flower spray, white petals wilting nearby, spread by an uncaring wind. I try to place them back near the stone and wonder at this, the simplest of memorials, dignified in its spectacular setting. New stone near old stone. A butcher's blade of a sea is shining from afar, sharpening itself against a stony sky.

* * *

Turning, I discover two types of mushroom, almost hidden, trodden on. The *Mycena haematopus* is an easy one to identify with its red tinge. I later find that the second is *Basidiomycetes*. In rockpools a stone's throw from this place, the orange-coloured sponge *Hymeniacidon* contains an anti-cancer compound.

* * *

Arriving home, I realise that Arthur's Stone has moved and gone before me. My mobile enables me to load it on my laptop screen. No physical ardour, no lift or tug of war, just a click and a trick of light. An easy transmission. Like Arthur, I throw my stone to friends across the water, enthusiasts such as Pamela Petro with her terrific, petrific name. She responds within seconds.

*   *   *

The mind moves with it in this, the most restless of times. Fragmented by sounds and waves, we want to go down to stonedepth and meditate, to grasp something in this rockpool beyond any googling or expedia-moves in the fast track of learning. Here we have to wait on stone, trust its inscape, its voicelessness.

*   *   *

This image on my screen is a reminder – much like the scan of a baby – that there is something there, inside, that is living.

GUARDING EMPTINESS

Tinkinswood Burial Chamber, South Glamorgan, Wales

Elin ap Hywel

We're not sure, to begin with, that we're in the right place. The 1950s Ancient and Historic Monuments-style fingerpost pointing the way to Tinkinswood indicates nothing more promising than a disaffected sheep. Pylons stalk the fields against an overcast sky. Their voices are the muted roar of descending and ascending aeroplanes at Cardiff Airport. The dead would be impressed. And the dead, after all, is why we are here. We soldier on regardless, over the tussocky grass.

A cowpat incident or two later, we come to the boundary of the site. Two significant-looking stones face each other across a wire fence like separated lovers. We enter through an incongruous turnstile. We are going to the fair.

Now we are encouraged by another sign. It reads: 'This site is in the care of Cadw Welsh Historic Monuments on behalf of the Secretary of State for Wales'. Someone has scratched out the last five words and written 'GODDESS' instead. There is something else sgraffitoed underneath. We puzzle over it for a while.

I decide it reads 'damned profaners'.

*   *   *

I know you only through two photographs. In the first you are standing in the doorway at Brynderw, wearing a Norfolk jacket and tie, your eyes level and shrewd above a hawk nose. Your father and mother sit on chairs in front of you, my grandmother dark-clothed, sagging a little but immaculately coiffed. Your sisters' hair, too, is done to within an inch of its life. They wear fitted, fully-fashioned jumpers, dirndl skirts and double ropes of cultured pearls. I may be biased, but with their shapely lips and racehorse legs they are beautiful, incongruous fashion plates against the bouldery, whitewashed farmhouse walls.

Two daughters and a son form a semi-circle around their sitting parents. This is the plan: the daughters go on to university, and marriage. You, your father's son, stay on and run the farm. It's looking good.

Taid wears a tweed suit and his habitual expression of sardonic intelligence. He has survived the Great War. He's taking nothing for granted.

*   *   *

Then we see the grove and the burial mound.

At first I'm disappointed. I last saw Tinkinswood on a primary school trip over thirty years ago. Rightly or wrongly, my memory has carpeted the woodland around and behind the monument with bluebells, a Disneyesque lake of heartbreaking blue. Now it's late September and the palette is muted. All the sedge has most certainly withered from the lake. Donkey-brown teazle heads straggle their floss over the sere stalks of other, unidentifiable plants. Apart from a white plastic bag caught in the branches of a tree, which I take, for a moment, to be a pair of enormous knickers (the Goddess's, maybe?), everything is grey, or brown, or green. No birds sing.

I am chary of recalling my last visit. The memory is hardly likely to be an accurate record of the way I thought when I was eleven years old. Apart from the bluebells, I mainly remember having our photograph taken by the teacher.

Andrea, Colin, Lynwen, Huw – for a second vanished children pose by the trees.

I have a definite impression, though, that on that day I took to the *twt*-ness of the burial chamber in a big way. It seemed to me then intimate, domestic rather than imposing, less a ship of death than a bijou pied-à-terre in immortality.

So it's surprising, this time around, to discover that it has the largest capstone of any monument in Britain. It's a giant's table, a warriors' dancefloor, an elemental hearthstone. What did the people who put it here fear, we wonder? That the living would break in? Or that the dead would get out?

*   *   *

The other – a small, black-and-white 1950s snapshot with a glossy white border – shows a young man like the sum total of all his male relations. A countryman, a man of practical action. Self-confident, capable, sure of his place in the world.

You loved motorbikes and once went with your friends to see the TT races on the Isle of Man.

One July day in 1954 you drove your motorbike out of the farm lane onto the main Bala to Corwen road. A car struck the bike. You were thrown and killed.

These are the only facts I know about you, apart from your initials, carved in the chunky dark oak of the family dresser.

*   *   *

It is pleasant being here alone, my friend and I. There's time to look closely at the herringbone pattern of the stones in the approach walls and notice the patches of colour nesting there: lichen, some turmeric-bright, some ghost-grey; and tiny pink stellar flowers, creeping. We notice the way the hawthorn bushes on the right drip garnet-coloured berries.

We debate, for a while, the names of the other trees, argue the difference between birch and beech. I lament our lack of Celtic tree lore. My friend takes photographs of the disputed leaves with her digital camera so that, later on, we can check. (Later we peer at them, then forget.)

And then we approach the monument. Its coat of earth flayed from it by archaeology and weather, Tinkinswood is a skinned rabbit. The pale brick pillar holding up one portion of the capstone is bald, incongruous. It bears the legend 'Excavated 1914'.

*　　*　　*

My grandfather enlisted in the Artists' Rifles in December 1916, went to war in May 1917, was wounded and spent some time in a military hospital in France. He returned home and married my grandmother: an ordinary story of extraordinary luck. I finger the brick and wonder what happened to the spadesmen and measurers of the 1914 dig, what other kinds of earth and stones passed through their fingers, hid their eyes, after Tinkinswood.

*　　*　　*

I imagine there will be evidence of recent activity or even habitation inside the mound: a burnt-out fire, maybe, empty cans of Blackthorn, discarded condoms. Someone – one of the goddess-worshippers, perhaps – has placed three tea lights on ledges in the rock. The wax has melted and set in sad white stalactites on the stone. I wonder what ritual this was: an invocation, a prayer, an equinox devotion? There is an aperture shaped like an arrowslit next to the candles: the effect is curiously, touchingly High Church.

We examine the stone of the roof more closely. It looks porous, like a stone colander. In one place there are five fingertip-sized holes made, my friend says, 'by someone trying to get out'. I laugh, and place the fingers of my left hand, one in each hole, as far in as I can reach. It feels dangerous and intimate, as if I am reaching inside the stone itself. My friend shudders.

As we had expected, the inside is full of – well, nothing; a lot of rather muddy and stony nothing.

No skeletons, no grave goods, no ghosts. The presence of their absence is palpable.

❊   ❊   ❊

On the opening page of the family bible there is an inscription recording the gift from Soar chapel to my grandfather, giving thanks for the Lord's guidance and protection over his life and character during his service in the Great War. On this page it is 1919. He is twenty nine years old; his life is a field in front of him.

In Nehemiah 4, it is 27 July 1954. I find the order of service for my uncle's funeral. The first page reads: *Mal lladron, dison y daw*. It comes in the night, like thieves.

❊   ❊   ❊

I have read about Tinkinswood, preparatory to today's visit. It belongs to the Cotswold-Severn style of Stone-Age tomb. Here, it seems, the remains of the dead were tangible evidence that the land was taken, that it belonged to the tribe. Some tombs were used for as long as five hundred years, half a millennium of generation on generation of dead doing what they were good at: protecting the land for their descendants.

There was no ordering of bodies in neat rows, no sense of individuality in death. The freshly dead were placed, it's thought, in a pit a little way from the burial mound, to decay until time and the weather revealed the bones beneath. Bone would lie on bone, fragment on fragment in a pile of ancestors, each clavicle and tibia a shout on the wind to invisible enemies: this land is ours.

I peer into the putative charnel pit. I try to imagine how it would feel to know that your mother or brother was lying here. Would you look? Would you want to? Would you be allowed?

❊   ❊   ❊

Shortly after that first visit to Tinkinswood I become avidly interested in ghost stories. Headless horsemen, white ladies and hairy hands which grab steering wheels, driving cars and occupants into some deathsome bog, replace ponies in my affections. At night my bedclothes are a torchlit bivouac against the forces of darkness as I devour accounts of poltergeists, corpse candles and phantom funerals. I am given a terrific row in the Welsh class for surreptitiously (but not surreptitiously enough) reading about the hauntings of North Devon under the desk when I should have been attending to aspirant mutations. It's a toss-up whether I am more scared by the ghosts of Bovey Tracey or by the fear that my mother will find out.

I become particularly interested in the pseudo-science of the paranormal, the machines for recording inaudible voices, the cameras for taking pictures of invisible ectoplasm. The people who stay all night in haunted houses, giving themselves up to whatever dread others live there. My favourite theory states that supernatural manifestations are drawn, above all, to houses where girls around the age of puberty live. It seems almost worth having periods in order to see a ghost.

In Maths I stare out of the window and imagine what it would be like really, truly, to meet a ghost. Sometimes they look, for the first few seconds, like a real person. How would I know what it was? By the sudden temperature drop to freezing which the books mention? By something about the figure itself? Perhaps part of it would be missing – its head (if it had been beheaded) or its legs below the knee (because of the rise in ground level over the centuries).

I could pass you in a crowd in town and never even know I'd seen your ghost. I half-thrill, half-terrify myself with these imaginings.

                    *   *   *

When you die there is no son to take over the farm. In time my grandparents give up farming and move to the village.

My grandmother stands at the window in Brynderw. She looks out at the rooks, the fields sodden with the thaw. 'The poor boy', she says. 'Oh, my poor boy.'

*   *   *

Things you can't ask your mother when you're eleven:
Do you believe in ghosts?
How does it feel when your brother dies?
Can I watch Record Breakers before I do my homework?
Does it hurt? Does it hurt a lot?

*   *   *

I am home from college. I am going out on a winter's morning but I can't find my mittens. My mother lends me a pair of supple black leather gloves with simple stitching.
'I like these', I say.
'I bought them for your uncle's funeral', she says. 'You can keep them.'
There is a silence while we think about this and I try to pull on the gloves. They are tiny and very tight: it's like trying to re-skin sausages. Nineteen and beautiful, I think, walking into Mrs Plack's emporium to buy a pair of gloves to wear to your brother's funeral.
By now the gloves are cutting off the circulation in my fingers. I am determined to wear them.

*   *   *

'We should probably sleep the night here', I tell my friend. 'To really get the atmosphere.'
Her look is enough. She doesn't actually have to say 'You're clean off your head'.
We settle for a coffee in Marks and Spencers at Culverhouse instead.

*   *   *

Was it the dresser or was it the back door of the farmhouse? The dresser is downstairs. I can go and check. Oh no, I can't, I remember. There are so many plates on it I won't be able to pull it away from the wall.

Nympsfield Long Barrow, Gloucestershire, England

Jem Poster

You use a pointing-trowel, a tool intended for an altogether different purpose. Over the months, the years, it adapts itself to your needs, its handle shaped by continual friction against your palm, its blade honed and burnished, unevenly worn. In the hands of a skilled archaeologist the trowel reads the earth like braille, picking up the tell-tale softening of disturbed soil where a drainage trench cuts across the site, the gritty scatter of crushed limestone around an eroded doorsill. The blade flickers over the exposed strata, scraping, peeling, probing. Shards and flakes, a dark organic stain against clean red clay, the gleam of bone laid bare: fragments of the past brought carefully to light.

*   *   *

April 1974. I'm working on the chambered tomb at Nympsfield, hunkered down out of the wind between the limestone slabs which form the sides of one of the burial chambers. Birdsong from the hedgerow, the sun warm on the skin of my neck and the back of my hands as I scrape away at the moist earth. I think I'm singing quietly to myself, but from this distance I can't hear the song.

I was on the archaeological circuit in those days, not so much charting a career for myself as drifting with unseen currents, comfortable with my own aimlessness and deeply, if naively, curious about my surroundings and discoveries. I'd worked on excavations from Cornwall to Orkney, and had spent the preceding winter in Yorkshire, first on the site of a deserted medieval village some ten miles east of York, and then in York itself, where I'd wrestled for six weeks with the stratigraphical complexities of a small patch of ground temporarily opened up by demolition on the south side of the city. I'd had enough of the cold and enough of urban archaeology, and the prospect of working in rural Gloucestershire as the days lengthened was more attractive to me than the offer of a long-term contract to continue where I was. Passing through Huntingdon on my way south, I disposed of my stained and tattered sheepskin jacket in a roadside bin and continued my journey with a sense of lightness, of expanded potential.

✳   ✳   ✳

Nympsfield chambered tomb is one of a small group of Neolithic burial mounds or barrows strung out along an escarpment overlooking the Severn Vale, a few miles from the Cotswold wool town of Stroud. Its design is broadly typical of megaliths of its place and period: vertical slabs – orthostats – form a series of compartments which the builders would have roofed with further slabs – capstones – before covering the entire construction with earth. At the east end, the entrance is marked by a sudden broadening of the structure in the form of two outward-curving drystone walls, the characteristic 'horns' of the monument. By 1974 the capstones were long gone from the Nympsfield tomb, though most of the orthostats and a substantial proportion of both horns remained. I remember or imagine myself running a hand across the weathered surface of one of the slabs, or teasing the crumbs of reddish soil from the interstices of the walling. I was drawn to such details, but I'm as interested now, from my present vantage-point, in those missing capstones.

It's not difficult to account for their absence. Funerary
monuments of this kind tend to suffer more from our
attention than from our neglect, and the Nympsfield barrow
has received more than its fair share of attention. After the
first recorded excavation of the site in 1862, the writer of the
report noted that the tomb 'appeared to have been opened on
a former occasion'. A range of finds from the mound-
material, including the neck of an early seventeenth-century
glass bottle and a George I halfpenny of 1723, suggest that
there may well have been more than one such occasion, and
there's no doubt at all that, by the time of the first modern
excavation there in 1937, the mound had been subjected to a
series of intrusions. What we were looking at in 1974 wasn't
simply the prehistoric record but a more complex picture,
created in part by our predecessors in the field: the
archaeologists of 1937 and, further back, the amateur
antiquarians whose work might be said to have laid the
foundations of modern archaeology.

The 1974 excavations lasted a month; some of those early
antiquarians, working with other enthusiasts or a few
labourers, could polish off a barrow in a day or less.
Sometimes considerably less: in his *Vestiges of the Antiquities
of Derbyshire*, the indefatigable nineteenth-century barrow-
digger, Thomas Bateman, offers an account of a particularly
busy day in May 1845, during which four adjacent mounds
were excavated. The passage offers a disturbing insight into
Bateman's practices: of the third barrow, he remarks that the
primary interment was not discovered, adding revealingly
that, in his view, 'the labourers (being left to themselves) were
not sufficiently careful in their researches, and overlooked it',
while the fourth barrow was also 'by no means satisfactorily
examined'. Nothing could be firmly established, he concludes
with the wisdom of hindsight, 'except a conviction of the impolicy
of attempting to explore so many barrows in one day'.

Bateman and his fellow antiquarians were able to work at
such speed because their aims were relatively simple and their
methods, by modern standards, extremely crude. Bateman's
primary interest lay in salvaging relics for his private

collection, and though he published a number of rudimentary plans alongside the finely engraved figures of artefacts discovered in the course of his investigations, all the evidence suggests that planning was not, for him, the priority it is for most modern archaeologists. For myself, I remember hours spent hunched over a strung grid, mapping out on draughtsman's film each subtle change in soil coloration, the varying levels of the exposed strata and the location of every bone, potsherd or flint flake. Just recently, revisiting the published report of the Nympsfield excavations and poring over the interior elevations of the orthostats, I had a brief but vivid flashback, perhaps to an actual moment, perhaps to something more generic: the drawing-board propped on my knees, the taut datum-line trembling in the spring wind as I measure and plot, with obsessive precision, the angular profile of the slabs.

*   *   *

The clearer and more comprehensive the record, the more authoritatively a site can be interpreted, not only by its excavators but also by those who come after them. Interpretation at Nympsfield is naturally hampered by the poverty of the pre-1937 record, but it's nevertheless possible, by sifting the evidence accumulated over the past hundred and fifty years, to arrive at a reasonably detailed understanding of the monument's construction. With the capstones in place and the earth piled above and around the chambers, the mound-material was consolidated by an overlay of loose limestone. Most of this appears to have been deposited more or less at random, but there's sporadic evidence of more careful placement: a sketchy run of neatly aligned stones, indicative rather than structural, appears to have defined the two long flanks of the barrow.

We can surmise a certain amount, too, about the use of the monument. At least seventeen individuals – men, women and children – are represented by the human bones recovered from the site, and it seems reasonable to infer from this, as from the presence of more than one type of Neolithic pottery, that the burials took place over a significant period of time. And although cremation wasn't the norm in the Neolithic period, there's evidence here that, in a few instances and not necessarily at the time of interment, the bones of the dead were exposed to fire.

But there's so much we can only guess at. Take, for example, the patch of burnt material shown on the 1937 plan as a circular feature lying a little outside the tomb entrance and equidistant between the horns: even if we were confident enough to ascribe a ritual significance to the fire it represents, we'd still be unable to say with any certainty what kind of ceremony had taken place in that charged liminal space. And even if we did know that, and even if we could discover a relationship between the ritual burning and the nearby scatter of potsherds, all derived from a single Neolithic vessel – even then, what access would we have to the thoughts and emotions of the participants? How could we understand – I mean understand feelingly and intimately – the nature of their grief, or of the consolations offered by their irrecoverable rites?

I suspect that what first attracted me to archaeology, and to prehistoric archaeology in particular, was precisely the riddling nature of its testimony. I was drawn not simply by its discoveries but by the sense of an uncharted hinterland, a space where the imagination might work with a degree of freedom. I was always more interested in accessing mysteries than in establishing facts. For all my meticulousness – the delicate trowel-work, the precise draughtsmanship – my approach was fundamentally unscientific and, in that respect, may have had more in common with that of the amateur antiquarian than I should have cared to admit at the time.

*   *   *

And in other respects too. Contemporary prehistorians have spoken scathingly about the damage caused by their barrow-rifling predecessors, but damage is, of course, inseparable from the whole business of excavation. Archaeology painstakingly reverses the processes of deposition, stripping back layer after layer in careful sequence; the more thorough the excavation, the more complete the destruction. We may have the detailed drawings, the labelled finds, a published report, and we may even have, as at Nympsfield, a partial reconstruction of the mound's contours; but none of that will bring back the lost substance of the thing itself. My meticulous procedures, it occurs to me, were an attempt to justify the inherently destructive enterprise; perhaps even a form of expiation for my own part in it.

Writing of damage, I unearth another memory, darker and more deeply buried than my recollections of Nympsfield. I'm twenty years old and working on a Bronze-Age barrow under the directorship of a man whose lack of archaeological expertise should have barred him from the job. His assistant is even less well qualified, a woman with almost no archaeological experience at all. We're lifting burial urns, beautiful incised vessels of coarse-textured brown clay, and storing them in the site hut.

What possesses the woman to start cleaning out the urns, hacking at the dense mass of cremated bone with a trowel, chipping and scouring, breaking at least one of the vessels in the process? Even at this distance in time, I feel the intrusion, the insult. You don't need to be an expert to recognise that this was bad archaeological practice: the damaging of finds, the contamination of samples, are self-evidently harmful. But the damage, I see now, was taking place at a more fundamental level.

Another site, another Bronze-Age barrow, this one precariously perched on the edge of an artificial cliff created by sand-quarrying. The quarry-owners have acted correctly in notifying the appropriate authorities and suspending their activities in the area; the site is being scrupulously excavated and recorded in advance of further quarrying. Its three dozen urns will be lifted intact from the mound; the calcined bone from each vessel will be examined under laboratory conditions and the analyst's findings published in a detailed report. Sound archaeological practice – but also a form of collusion. I don't think it would have crossed my mind at the time that I might have taken an active stand against the destruction of the heathland and its ancient burial-places, but within a few years I would find myself gripped by a deep unease about the very nature of the work I was engaged in. When, in the mid-1980s, I withdrew from archaeology, it was with a measure of relief at the thought that I should no longer have to disturb the bones of the buried dead.

*   *   *

The flow runs both ways: we disturb these bones and the monuments that enclose them – often, it seems, under some imperfectly understood compulsion – and they, in turn, disturb us. There was a local belief that the stone chambers at Nympsfield were the remains of a lazar-house, and that anyone approaching them ran the risk of being infected with leprosy. Folk-tales cluster around sites of this kind – stories of fairies and goblins, devils and witches, ghosts and giants; of mysterious music and hollow groans; of stones that resist being moved or, if moved, return to their proper places in defiance both of their disturbers and the laws of nature. One particularly detailed story, relating to a burial-site not far from Nympsfield, describes how two men discover a doorway which gives them access to the chambers of the tomb. There they find a collection of urns, some containing ashes and others full of coins; but they also encounter a guardian in the form of an armoured figure who sits with a lamp burning in front of him, in the company of two embalmed human heads. At the approach of the intruders, he smashes the lamp to smithereens. As the pair beat a hasty retreat, the tomb collapses behind them, burying their discoveries and preventing subsequent access.

To observe that few of these stories could possibly be true is at once to state the obvious and to miss the point. The truths they embody are imaginative rather than narrowly factual, intuitively conceived rather than rationally established. Collectively, they register the power of these sacred places, and the unsettling vibrations which resonate outward from them through time and space. In 1975 John Piper, an artist acutely receptive to such influences, made studies of two Pembrokeshire megaliths, Carreg Samson and Pentre Ifan. Everything about these images bespeaks a restless, brooding energy: the sweeping or swirling patterns within and around the stones' unstable outlines, the multiple perspectives held within a single frame, the shadowy washes dramatically broken by shafts or blocks of light. Piper's images are not accurate in the way that the plans and elevations of the same sites in *Archaeologia Cambrensis* are accurate, but it would be a very odd judgement indeed that pronounced them less true to their subject.

Another story, this one from the pages of the *Wiltshire Archaeological and Natural History Magazine* for December 1944. It's told by B. H. Cunnington, a Fellow of the Society of Antiquaries of Scotland, who, nearly forty years earlier, had assisted his wife in the excavation of the unusually richly furnished burial discovered in the Bronze-Age barrow at Manton, near Marlborough. After the excavations, a local resident complained to her doctor that she was being troubled by an elderly woman who came from the site each night and walked around her cottage, peering into the windows. Urged by his patient to give her something to keep the unwelcome visitor away, the doctor said he would send her a bottle of medicine, which she was to drink after dark before going upstairs, without a light, and getting into bed. The remedy appears to have been successful: after a few nights, the haunting came to an end.

What intrigues me about this tale is a secondary narrative glimpsed somewhere in the background, a narrative of overlapping perspectives at a transitional point in our cultural history. The patient seems to belong fairly unambiguously to an older, less sceptical order, but how does the doctor understand his role? – as traditional exorcist or as modern psychotherapist? And what are we to make of Cunnington's introductory paragraph, which leads us to the ghost story by way of a factual reference to the human remains discovered in the barrow: 'The late Dr. Beddoe', he says, 'was of the opinion the skeleton was that of a female of considerable age, and this is borne out by the following story told me by the late Dr. J. B. Maurice, of Marlborough'. I had to return to the second half of that sentence to make sure I hadn't misread it. I hadn't: Cunnington is adducing the age and gender of the ghost as evidence supportive of Dr Beddoe's scientific conclusions. The remark is casual, even perhaps half-inadvertent, and – given its placing in the pages of a mid-twentieth-century archaeological journal – almost as disconcerting as the story it introduces.

* * *

September 2005, and I'm travelling north from Bristol on the M5. Rain and spray, a strong, gusting wind. As I slow to take the Stroud exit I see, on the southbound carriageway, the jittery play of blue lights around the scene of an accident, the static tailback behind. I'm in sombre mood as I approach my destination, the engine groaning on the long climb out of Frocester.

'Nympsfield Long Barrow' say the brown roadsigns, but the signboard that greets you as you swing off the road announces that you are entering the Coaley Peak picnic area. A vast, deserted car park and, beyond that, an expanse of trim grassland, more lawn than meadow, evidently maintained by the local council. As I draw up I can see the barrow through the spattered side-window of the car, a little blister on the lip of the scarp some fifty yards to the north.

The wind tugs at the car door as I open it, but the rain is easing. I strike off across the wet grass towards the mound, and it comes to me as I walk that I used to approach it from some other angle; but when I try to retrieve the details – a five-barred gate presents itself, a trodden path – I find nothing I can be sure of.

And the mound itself is lower than I remember, the slabs more raggedly irregular, the chambers narrower. Within the chambers, and in the space between the horns, the ground has been strewn with coarse gravel. What I recall as gaps in the structure, at its northern, southern and western extremities, have been filled in with modern drystone walling. Less obviously – indeed, I know this only because it's mentioned in the excavation report – the visible sections of the horns are also of modern construction: four courses of drystone cladding built in front of the original structure to mimic and protect it.

None of this is surprising. What stops me in my tracks is a line of ash trees and a pair of beeches growing where, if memory serves, our site-hut stood during the period of the excavations. These trees, I realise, weren't here in 1974. They're not fully mature, but they're sturdy and substantial, the largest ash more than twenty feet in height; and for me, as I stand beneath the dripping boughs, they speak of the passage of time more directly, more intimately and more disquietingly than the monument they overlook.

The rain is strengthening again, whipping in across the flood-plain from the west. I make my way to the edge of the scarp and stare into the murk, my face stinging. I remember the whole expanse shining in April sunlight, my gaze drawn out over the Severn to the long line of the Welsh hills beyond. Intricate patterning of fields, lanes and boundaries, the sheen of the widening river: such clarity, such luminous scope. This morning I can barely make out the valley floor below me.

*   *   *

'Today', wrote John Piper in 1939, watching hikers larking carelessly beneath the looming masses of Gordale Scar, 'no terror.' There would be terrors enough of our own making in the months and years that followed, but the implicit point of Piper's notebook jotting – that humankind risks losing the sense of awe proper to its encounters with a world of inhuman grandeur and impenetrable mystery – was valid then, as it is now. The scoured, sanitised remains of the Nympsfield barrow seem emblematic of lost or attenuated relationship, their conservation the hollow gesture of an imaginatively impoverished age. *Approach at your peril*, says the old tale of the lazar-house. *Come in*, says the local council, *and bring a picnic*.

The gibe is too easy. I don't subscribe to a neatly dualistic view of such matters: the truffling antiquarians of the eighteenth and nineteenth centuries were not, after all, the first grave-robbers and, conversely, our own protective legislation isn't completely unconnected with the taboos which kept the tillers' ploughshares respectfully skirting, year on year, century after century, the dangerous citadels of the fairy-folk. Even so, it's arguable that, as a culture, we stand at a greater distance than any of our predecessors from certain sources of psychological or spiritual sustenance, and that a reductive materialism is at once cause and effect of that distance. The diagnostic rim-sherd and the carbon-dated charcoal sample may tell us less than we think, less than we need to know.

*   *   *

A summer evening towards the end of the last century. A remote barrow, untended, perhaps unlooted; a solitary foot-traveller standing in long grass a little apart from the mound, breathing the soft scent of gorse flowers and the sharper odours sent up by the bruised vegetation at his feet; a nightjar calling from neighbouring woodland. If it weren't for the traveller's modern clothing and the vapour-trails traced across the fading sky above him, the scene might be described as timeless.

It comes as if borne on the air with the heath-smells, a sudden, dizzying intimation of unseen immensities, of imaginative possibility. The vision, if it can be called that, sets the traveller trembling. He doesn't turn, though, but holds his ground, riding out the tremors until they pass. He stands there for a long time, watching the shadows deepen around the barrow, obscurely moved by some notion of lives lived with renewed reverence; of people stepping delicately around such sites, giving them their due, letting them be.

Burial Chamber, Samson Hill, Bryher, The Isles of Scilly

David Constantine

B ryher is an island about a mile long and, at most, half a mile wide. The name means 'place of hills'. There are half a dozen of them and Samson Hill is the most southerly. It looks out over perhaps five hundred yards of water to the uninhabited island of Samson, which is itself composed of two very striking hills.

There is general agreement that until well into historical times, perhaps even as late as the eleventh century, much of the archipelago of the Scillies, perhaps all but St Agnes out on a watery limb to the south-west, was joined in one island. A glance at a map showing sea-depths makes this seem very likely. Bryher at that time, and Samson with it, no doubt, was the notably hilly north-western border of quite a large island that took in present-day Tresco, St Helen's, Tean, St Martin's, the Eastern Isles and St Mary's. Most of the land within that perimeter was low-lying; then wind-blown sand, then the incoming Atlantic, covered over its fields and wells and hearths. The dozens of chamber tombs for which Scilly is famous were built on the hills and the sea has not reached them, yet.

There are at least three tombs on Samson Hill. The one I love best, that haunts me most, is on a ledge, a sort of platform, on the southern slope. Many and various are the ways to come at it, each beautiful and always surprising. My favourite lately has been a path up through the ferns and the gorse of the steep north side. As you climb, as you begin to feel the bulk and the shape of the hill, the way passes between two very large stones, megaliths themselves, that make a portal. You are entering upon something.

Samson Hill is an excellent place for gathering gorse stubs, to fuel the winter fires; also for counting your blessings, in a panorama of three hundred and sixty degrees; and at night for thanking your lucky stars. Stand in the centre of the hill, on the summit, and there's a tomb to the right of you and another to the left of you, and between them, but some distance further forward where the ground begins to descend, there's a single upright stone, waist-high, rather wedge-shaped; and this apex of a triangle made by it and the two summit tombs is the pointer to the best still to come: the tomb on the ledge below you, on the southern slope.

There are two outcrops of granite, and between them, making the second of three steps down a line, is the tomb in question, on its platform. You get the first view of it from the edge of the first rocky outcrop. Into it, I should say. From that vantage point you look down into the black hole of a tomb that has been there for perhaps three-and-a-half-thousand years. Not in that condition, of course. For most of its existence it had the usual form of chamber tombs on Scilly: a circle of kerbstones around a low oblong chamber massively walled and roofed, the whole thing under a raised barrow of earth. Of this particular edifice, the mound has gone, the encircling kerbstones and the chamber are still there, but only four or five of the slabs that made the roof of the chamber have remained where they were set; a couple in the middle have been dislodged, leaving a gap. So from above you see diagonally through the opened roof, into what was the most secret place. That place looks black.

Climb down and you can do all the things one might usually do to try to get near the spirit of such a site: circle it very laboriously around its outer rim through gorse and brambles; crawl into it, stretch out or curl up in it. Or best, perhaps, sit quiet on the perch it makes and look across at the island of Samson.

Sea, where there were fields; a sea that is almost always running fast before a south-westerly breeze, a sea whose colours won't stay still but shift under the weather and according to the depth of tide from charcoal black through slate blue-grey, to startling green, lapis-lazuli and turquoise. Flecked white, the waves come on and on like the hexameters of an endless epic, inexhaustibly varying the constant line. If you sit there at night, under stars and a moon that seem to sheer away through the clouds at a frightful speed, you are at the apex of the beams of two lighthouses, Peninnis, on St Mary's, and the Bishop, far out on its rock. The Bishop particularly, there being nothing but water between you and it, seems to single you out. Once you know the place, the other lighthouses, as far away as the Lizard, as near as Round Island, will be invisibly present within the observation chamber of your skull. You can feel them signalling. Lighthouses are a benign human invention, and a chamber tomb, particularly one perched on a platform, is a fine place to take in their usefulness and beauty.

It is like being on the sea itself, which is all around, and the platform raised up not far above it, like a captain's bridge. Several of the oblong chambers in Scilly, within their circles, actually have the shape of a boat. The circle itself might be a coracle, and the lying-down place inside it is often shaped with a bow and stern. This feeling is intensified at the tomb on Samson Hill because of the triple stepping-down, like decks, of outcrop, tomb and outcrop. Truly, it feels as though the hill itself is faring forward, pushing through the sea.

The ship of death is a common and well-founded image; seaworthy, you might call it, fit, necessary. At about the time of the building of this tomb on Bryher, it was customary in Ancient Egypt to equip the dead with a model of the boat they would need for their afterlife. In Lawrence's *Last Poems* there must be a dozen sketches towards or around his 'Ship of Death', as though he were working at the ship itself, fitting it out 'with all accoutrements' for 'the long journey towards oblivion'. Think for a while, and one such vessel after another shapes up in the mind. Images survive because we cannot do without them. Of course, it is comforting to think of the dead sailing into an afterlife, taking with them things they loved in life, particular ornaments, and things they might need where they are going to, their cooking pots and tools. Consolatory, for the living, to wish the dead bon voyage. But in a sense we go with them, we ride upon them, they are a vessel for us. That would be a good, perhaps the best, aspiration in life: to become a vessel in death, a ship, for your loved ones to fare forward in. Something fit, serviceable, able to be steered and sailed wherever they have to travel, for their own course of life, as far as Brendan if they like, as far as Pytheas. The dead themselves, of their own volition, are going nowhere. So it is easy to reverse the conceit – it is only a conceit, but it might be made effective – and say that we, the living, are the vessel, we carry the dead forward, we continue them, they live on in the shape of the life we make. One way or another the sense is clear: the dead are vital, we cannot do without them, and we are vital to them, they have no life but through us.

I wrote a first draft of this essay on Amorgos, in the eastern Cyclades, and am finishing it now on Bryher. There are several connections between Scilly and the Greek islands, and not just in my head. The tomb on Samson Hill looks out to the quite shallow water under which still lie the two separated halves of the *Colossus*, wrecked in December 1799 and taking down with her much of Sir William Hamilton's second collection of Greek vases. They brought up thousands of sherds in the 1960s and a couple of years ago a beautiful figurehead from the poopdeck. The tomb, understood as a prow, points towards the twin hills of Samson Island, each of which is embossed with similar tombs. Those on the south hill are joined together by a massive wall, a wall along the spine that threads the tombs together like giant beads, a wall that has always reminded me of Tiryns and Mycenae, a surviving massiveness, something beached now on a very remote shore of time, not readily intelligible, flotsam from an elsewhere. All so strange! Samson Hill, good for fuel, for the stars, for present gratitude, is also a very powerful reminder of how strange things are, how odd and uncanny life is, how many incommensurables are littered around in close proximity. I remember the shock of pleasure it gave me many years ago, reading about Greece, to learn that the Aegean Archipelago should be seen as a submerged land, its islands the still emergent peaks. Then to read Hölderlin's 'Patmos', with its imagery of necessary passage between 'the peaks of time' – by boat from island to island, by memory and imagination from age to age, to and fro, as though to pollinate, between the living and the dead.

Scilly is rich in images of loss and resurgence. The images are facts. A man goes into the water and is never seen again. Close to home, there within the embrace of terra firma, in the safe lagoon, he falls and vanishes. The tide that goes out fast takes him away. Fire went over Chapel Downs on St Martin's. Next spring there was a flowering of ten thousand foxgloves, whose seeds no one had known about.

The tides are big in Scilly. On the ebb the centre empties, all the low land within the broken rim of hills drains very shallow and in many places dry. Then the old wading routes, even the ancient dryshod routes, are remembered, seem negotiable, look riskily practicable again. Things surface as they do out of a consciousness far larger than the individual when the individual sleeps and dreams. So much loss and recovery in Scilly. The sea gives, takes, gives again. The vast Atlantic floods in on a storm, rips off a surface, scours a cliff face, and an old dwelling, a cist grave, its pots and bones, see the light of day. Then the sands move, and things recorded ten years ago, you will not find them now. Even under water the process of burying continues. The *Colossus* had to be located under drifts of sand. And year on year, even without global warming, very gently and inexorably the sea is rising. Samson Flats at low tide were discovered by William Borlase in the eighteenth century to be a place of wondrous disappearance. He noted the drystone walls going down into the sand. That departure, like creatures setting off into the underworld, is most remarkable on Samson, but all the islands have some such pointer downwards, towards what now lies under the bed of the central lagoon. There is an equivalent even on dry land: the fields, once cultivated, now abandoned and gone under depths of deep green and breezily agitated bracken, field after field overwhelmed, for some years the white narcissi in their season still showing through, until bracken takes all. There are half a dozen such fields, like an advance guard of the sea, under the tomb on Samson Hill.

Just above those fields, on the hillside just to the left of the tomb as you look out, there's a little apple tree. I don't know how it got there; it's not a survivor of any hedge. The fruit, not surprisingly in the salt winds, is rather meagre and bitter. But the very existence of an apple tree in such a place is a poignant fact and the blossom in spring is like a frail insistence. Ruins – the tomb is a ruin – have a present beauty and pathos more or less independent of their original aura and function. Now in October the tomb on Samson Hill is decorated around and below with sprigs of brilliant scarlet rosehips and wreathed with the little tongues of yellow gorse that summer and winter never stop. And apart from briar roses, it will have quite a thicket of foxgloves next year when the time comes. And summer and winter unfailingly there is the sea, the agitated quickness of water so close that with a following wind and a strong arm you could fling an apple into it. And further out, towards the Bishop and beyond, there are colossal effects: shafts of rainbow; ghostly dark bodies of advancing rain; light slanting down through cloud-holes, stiff as swords; and pools of light, liquid upon liquid, like molten lead or sheets of quicksilver on the water. And so on, truly without end, because even a generically identical effect is never the same in its practice, since light, wind, sea, the incalculably rapid and subtle makers, cannot keep still. The tomb, in its immediate environs and in its outlook, is a place of the greatest possible liveliness.

The builders set these places on the hills, on flat summits, on ridges, on slopes that overlooked. They did well. The tombs proved safer than houses. Houses and fields went under the sands and the sea. The tombs have survived.

I have been calling them tombs, but there are experts who

do not think them tombs at all; or not only tombs. Several of these quite capacious edifices have shown, on being opened, no evidence of human burial; or some such evidence, but as much, or more, of a deliberate depositing of materials having to do with the hope and efforts of continued human living. Handfuls of topsoil, for example; scrapings from the floor of a home; portions from a midden. Borlase, opening a barrow on Buzza Hill, St Mary's, in 1752, found 'no bones, nor urns, but some strong unctuous earth which smelt cadaverous'. As though he held in his hands, and sniffed at, a rich tilth, for seeding. It seems possible that these chambered cairns – the preferred name, if you hold this view – may indeed have accommodated first the ashes of some perhaps particularly revered person, but thereafter may have become a place more like a repository or a shrine, to which the dwellers on the fields below climbed with offerings suggestive or hopeful of continued life on earth.

I like that idea: a neighbourly place that you look up to, climb to, concentrate your feelings on; landmark, sign; the collecting of potency in a precinct close at hand. Shipman Head Downs, at the north end of Bryher, has dozens of cairns, crouched quite low in the tough heather, several of them linked by walls. That hill, like Gweal in the west with its half dozen cairns, is visible from Samson Hill. From island to island these upland places, none more than a hundred-and-thirty feet above the sea, are visible. The eye and the mind connect them, make a sort of surviving community of them, above the water that has isolated them.

The field walls below the tomb are, like the tomb, made of the substance of Samson Hill. And they are badged and tressed the same with old-gold and grey-green lichens. So are the abandoned dwellings, the tombs and the walls of Samson Island. Same substance, the granite, same texture and appearance. Looked at from below, particularly sideways and from below, this tomb on the hillside is not distinguishable from the outcrops of granite between which, on a platform, it stands. The bracken, gorse, brambles, wild roses and numerous flowers inhabit and rise around them all. The tomb and the walls of the abandoned fields below it might, from their appearance, be coeval. Indeed, the walls linking the cairns on Shipman Head Downs or on the hills of the Island of Samson are very hard to date; they might well belong in time with the vanishing field systems on the flats. And in any case, stones from one structure migrate to another – there is a movement of granite stones of varying sizes from place to place and from function to function. A perched block dumped by the glaciers looks much like the top of an outcrop so weathered as to be almost undercut and toppling. And both resemble the makings, particularly the disturbed or shattered makings, of a chamber tomb or cairn.

This relatedness, this tendency to revert to origins and first appearance (the substance of a hill), constitutes a dimension of timelessness; or of a time in which all ages, functions, kinds of life, partake or will partake. The dead are literally coeval, and by connecting with them, being their vessel, sailing their ship of death further into more and more life, we share in a dimension which, at the very least, may be said to exceed the self with all its accidents and peculiarities.

The chamber is a place of intensest concentration. Ashes in an urn in a chamber, tightly housed like that, are like the incipient leaf in a bud, the seeds in a flower head. A poem works similarly. Reaching out from a place as definite as the tomb on Samson Hill, it enters a dimension larger than the writer's self, larger than a generation, as large as all the ages of the human race. Particularity comes first – there is no poem, no life, without it – but the aspiration is to extend beyond that and enter into a lively coexistence with a universe which, though still human (since we apprehend it), might include the night sky strewn with stars and the earth packed with who knows what powers of sudden florescence. The cairn and chamber on the ledge over the rising sea, a place which, so it seems, human beings fed with their hopes of continuance on earth, have the concentration of a good poem. They release the imagination like seeds from a bursting poppy head. And as we are now, unless we imagine something better, and unless we act on it, our bits of terra firma will soon lose heart and will refuse to flower.

Locating the Megaliths in Wales

Presaddfed Burial Chamber
Ynys Môn

Platform Cairn
Brenig, Denbighshire

**Y Fuwch a'r Llo /
The Cow and Calf Standing Stones**
Pendam Mountain, Ceredigion

Pentre Ifan Burial Chamber
Pembrokeshire

**Stone Row, Parc y Meirw /
The Field of the Dead**
Llanllawer, Pembrokeshire

**Arthur's Stone /
Maen Ceti Burial Chamber**
Gower

Tinkinswood Burial Chamber
South Glamorgan

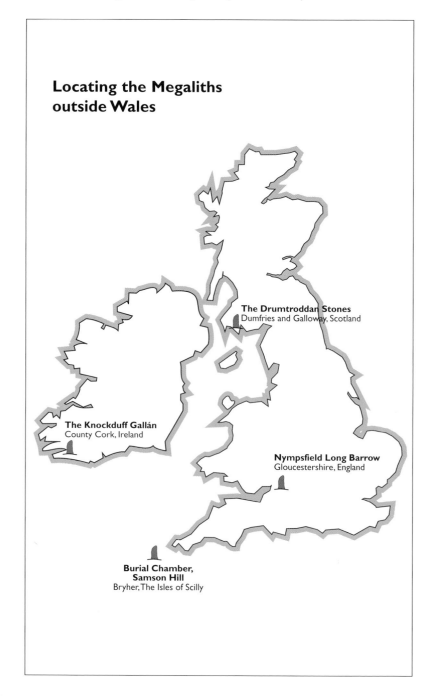

**Locating the Megaliths
outside Wales**

The Drumtroddan Stones
Dumfries and Galloway, Scotland

The Knockduff Gallán
County Cork, Ireland

Nympsfield Long Barrow
Gloucestershire, England

**Burial Chamber,
Samson Hill**
Bryher, The Isles of Scilly

MAP REFERENCES

Unless noted otherwise, grid references refer to the numbered Ordnance Survey 1:50,000 scale 'Landranger' maps.

The Drumtroddan Stones, Dumfries and Galloway, Scotland
OS 83; NX 364443

The Knockduff Gallán, County Cork, Ireland
OS Ireland, Discovery Series 79, W 225977 (now destroyed)

Presaddfed Burial Chamber, Anglesey / Ynys Môn, Wales
OS 114; SH 347809

Platform Cairn, Brenig, Denbighshire, Wales
OS 116; SH 989565

Y Fuwch a'r Llo / The Cow and Calf Standing Stones, Pendam Mountain, Ceredigion, Wales
OS 135; SN 723833

Pentre Ifan Burial Chamber, Pembrokeshire, Wales
OS 145; SN 099370

Stone Row, Parc y Meirw / The Field of the Dead, Llanllawer, Pembrokeshire, Wales
OS 157; SM 999359

Arthur's Stone / Maen Ceti Burial Chamber, Gower, Wales
OS 159; SS 491906

Tinkinswood Burial Chamber, South Glamorgan, Wales
OS 171; ST 092733

Nympsfield Long Barrow, Gloucestershire, England
OS 162; SO 794013

Burial Chamber, Samson Hill, Bryher, The Isles of Scilly
OS 203; SV 878142

BIOGRAPHICAL NOTES

ELIN AP HYWEL is a poet, editor and translator. Her books include *Ffiniau / Borders* (with Grahame Davies; Gomer, 2002) and (as editor) *Power: An Anthology of Short Stories by Women from Wales* (Honno, 1998). Her poems and translations have been widely anthologised, most recently in *The Bloodaxe Book of Modern Welsh Poetry* (2003). She currently shares a Royal Literary Fund Writing Fellowship at the University of Wales, Aberystwyth with Menna Elfyn. Having been shown many ancient stones over the years by friends, boyfriends and family (usually in the rain), she welcomes this opportunity to strike back.

GILLIAN CLARKE has published eight collections of poetry. She also writes plays and short stories, and translates Welsh poetry and fiction. She is president of Tŷ Newydd, the Writers' Centre in Gwynedd, which she co-founded in 1990, and is a part-time tutor in Doctoral Studies in Creative Writing at the University of Glamorgan. Recent books include *Collected Poems* (1997) and *Making the Beds for the Dead* (2004), both published by Carcanet. She lives in Ceredigion, Wales.

DAVID CONSTANTINE has published half a dozen volumes of poetry, most recently *Collected Poems* (Bloodaxe, 2004) and a volume of short stories, *Under the Dam* (Comma Press, 2005). He is the biographer of Sir William Hamilton and a translator of Goethe, Hölderlin, Kleist and Brecht. With his wife Helen he edits the magazine *Modern Poetry in Translation*. He first visited the Scillies in 1967 and has been there very often since, latterly for quite long periods.

MENNA ELFYN is the author of eight volumes of poetry. Her most recent collection is *Perffaith Nam* (Gomer, 2005), which will appear in Welsh–English parallel text in her *Selected Poems* (Bloodaxe, 2007). She has also written plays for stage, radio and television, and novels for children. In 2002 she was made *Bardd Plant Cymru* – Children's Poet Laureate of Wales. She is Writing Director of the Masters Programme in Creative Writing at Trinity College, Carmarthen and is Royal Literary Fund Fellow at the University of Wales, Aberystwyth. Her work has been translated into eighteen languages.

NIALL GRIFFITHS lives at the foot of Pendam mountain in mid-Wales. He has written five novels – *Grits* (2000), *Sheepshagger* (2001), *Kelly + Victor* (2002), *Stump* (2003) and *Wreckage* (2005), all published by Cape – and more shorter fiction, articles, reviews, travel pieces and radio plays than he cares to count.

TRISTAN HUGHES was born in Atikokan, Canada, and now lives on Anglesey / Ynys Môn, Wales. He won the Rhys Davies Short Story Prize in 2002 and is the author of two novels, *The Tower* (2003) and *Send My Cold Bones Home* (2006), both published by Parthian. He has given readings of his work at various international festivals, from New York to Prague. The relationship between identity and place is an enduring concern of his writing, both creative and critical.

ANDREW MCNEILLIE was born in 1946 at Hen Golwyn, Clwyd and educated at the primary school there and at John Bright Grammar School in Llandudno. He read English at Magdalen College, Oxford, and is currently Literature Editor at Oxford University Press. His collection of poems *Nevermore* (2000), in the Carcanet Oxford Poets series, was shortlisted for the Forward Prize for Best First Collection; *Now, Then* in the same series appeared in 2002. *An Aran Keening*, an account of his year-long sojourn on Inis Mór, 1968–69, was published in 2001 by the Lilliput Press, Dublin. A collection of poems, *Slower*, appeared from Carcanet in 2006.

BERNARD O'DONOGHUE was born in Cullen, County Cork, Ireland in 1945 and he still spends part of the year there. He moved to Manchester in 1962, and since 1965 he has lived in Oxford where he is Fellow in Medieval English at Wadham

College. He has published five books of poems, of which the most recent is *Outliving* (Chatto and Windus 2003). He has also published books and essays on medieval literature, and his translation of *Sir Gawain and the Green Knight* will be published in Penguin Classics in 2006.

JIM PERRIN, in his youth one of the most notable rock-climbers in Britain, was born in Manchester and has lived in Wales for over forty years. He has written two biographies, *Menlove* (Ernest Press, 1985) and *The Villain* (Hutchinson, 2005) – both of which won the Boardman Tasker Award for Mountaineering Literature, the latter also winning the Mountain History Award at Banff Mountain Festival 2005 – as well as five collections of essays, a best-selling book on Snowdonia, and *River Map* (Gomer, 2001), an essay on love and landscape. *The Guardian*'s Country Diarist for Wales, he contributes regular travel essays to the *Daily Telegraph* and monthly columns to *Climber* and *TGO* magazines.

JEM POSTER is the author of a collection of poetry, *Brought to Light* (Bloodaxe, 2001), and two novels, *Courting Shadows* (Sceptre, 2002) and *Rifling Paradise* (Sceptre, 2006). Other publications include a study of the poetry of the 1930s and a selection of George Crabbe's poetry. He holds the Chair of Creative Writing in the English Department at the University of Wales, Aberystwyth, and is a regular reviewer of new fiction for *The Guardian*.

DAMIAN WALFORD DAVIES, for whom megaliths have long been an obsession, is Senior Lecturer in the English Department at the University of Wales, Aberystwyth. He is the author of *Presences that Disturb: Models of Romantic Identity in the Literature and Culture of the 1790s* (2002) and the editor of *Echoes to the Amen: Essays After R. S. Thomas* (2003) and of the prose works of Waldo Williams (2001), all published by University of Wales Press. *Whiteout*, a volume of poetry (with Richard Marggraf Turley), will appear from Parthian in 2006.

ACKNOWLEDGEMENTS

Gomer Press is indebted to the following for the photographs included in this collection:

View of the Southern Stone, Drumtroddan (p. 8), © Martin McCarthy, Theasis.

A view of Caherbarnagh from the space where the Knockduff gallán once stood (p. 22), © Bernard O'Donoghue.

Presaddfed Burial Chamber (p. 30), Cadw. Crown copyright.

Platform Cairn, Brenig (p. 42), © Steve Gray (www.cistercian-way.newport.ac.uk).

Y Fuwch a'r Llo / The Cow and Calf (p. 54), © Damian Walford Davies.

Pentre Ifan Burial Chamber (p. 66), © David Wilson Photography.

Stone Row, Parc y Meirw (p. 76), © Chris Collyer (www.stone-circles.org.uk).

King Arthur's Stone (p. 86), © Graham Alcock (www.images-of-gower.co.uk)

Tinkinswood Burial Chamber (p. 92), Cadw. Crown copyright.

Nympsfield, Long Barrow (p. 100), © Celia Haddon (www.celiahaddon.co.uk)

Burial Chamber, Samson Hill (p. 112), © David Constantine.

Lines from Louis MacNeice's 'The Cromlech' are quoted by permission of David Higham Associates Ltd.